COMMUNICATING CHRIST TO THE CULTS

by

John Thomas Rogers

Regular Baptist Press
1300 North Meacham Road
Post Office Box 95500
Schaumburg, Illinois 60195

Library of Congress Cataloging in Publication Data

Rogers, John Thomas, 1955-
  Communicating Christ to the cults.

  1. Apologetics—20th century. 2. Witness bearing (Christianity) 3. Cults. 4. Mormon Church—Doctrinal and controversial works. I. Title.
BT1240.R63   1983   239   83-4421
ISBN 0-87227-091-2

© 1983
Regular Baptist Press
Schaumburg, Illinois
Printed in U.S.A.
All rights reserved

This book is not dedicated to the scholar who knows his Bible backward and forward theologically and is therefore ready to tackle any error, but rather to the inexperienced Christian who does not know what to say, but very desperately wants to share Christ with those who believe in "another Jesus."

Contents

Foreword	7
Acknowledgments	9
Introduction	11
1. Attitudes	15

Love • A Knowledge of the Bible

2. The Discussion *Part 1*	21

What about 2 John 9, 10? • Opening Comments • Establish Authority • Bible Cult • The Book of Mormon • The New World Translation • Non-Bible Cult

3. The Discussion *Part 2*	31

Define Terms • Use Terms That Work • Zero in on Salvation • What Actually Saves Us? • Closing Comments • Outline of Discussion

4. Authority of the Bible	47

Bible • Priesthood

5. The Nature of God	55

God • Holy Spirit • Jehovah • Jesus Christ • Trinity

6. The Way of Salvation	65

Baptism • Baptism for the Dead • Children of God • Eternal Security • Salvation—Works vs. Grace

7. Other Areas	83

Eternal Marriages • Lost Tribes of Israel • One Hundred anf Forty-four Thousand • Preexistence • Reincarnation • Soul Sleep: Eternity vs. Annihilation

8. Practical Helps 95
    Temporary Alternative to Discussion •
    Proper Use of Anti-Cult Material • Suggested Visitation Passages • The Bible as
    far as Translated Correctly • Point of No
    Discussion • Ephesians 2:8 and 9 and the
    Mormons • John 1:1 and the Jehovah's
    Witnesses
9. Why Witness to Religious People? 105
10. Appendix 107
    Letters to Mormons

Foreword

Normally, in a teacher-student relationship, the teacher by definition teaches and the student learns. But with John Rogers I found the situation to be reversed many times. In this particular situation, the instructor learned as much as the student. John was found to be a bottomless resource of information about Mormonism. He probably has a better grasp of Mormonism and its teaching than do ninety-five percent of all Latter-day Saints.

Despite his young age, John is well qualified by study and thousands of hours of witnessing to Mormons and other cultists to write this book.

I highly recommend this book—not just to be read, but to also be applied. Read it! Study it! Absorb it! Then wait until the Lord leads two smartly dressed, young, bike-riding men to knock on your door and put its contents to use.

Martin R. Dahlquist
Academic Dean
Spurgeon Baptist Bible College
Mulberry, Florida

Acknowledgments

It is impossible to give credit to everyone who helped prepare me for the writing of this book—there have been so many. A few deserve special mention: My mom and dad, who first started me studying the Bible when I was seven; Lloyd and Martha Larkin, the missionaries in Utah I worked under as an apprentice missionary (without whom I might never have sensed my burden for the Mormons). Then there is Martin Dahlquist, my college theology teacher, a man who has a talent for putting the difficult into understandable language. One individual I cannot forget to mention is my loving wife who stood by me and encouraged me as I wrote this book during the impossible period of missionary deputation. I also want to thank Mrs. Edwin Chapin for proofreading this manuscript and offering her excellent suggestions. I also wish to thank Mrs. Helen Lampe for typing the final manuscript. Finally, I wish to thank the Lord Jesus Christ, the One Who gives purpose and meaning to this book.

Introduction

You are sitting in your living room reading a book. There is a knock at your door. You rise to answer it, and in doing so you notice through the window two bicycles parked in the driveway. Opening the door, you discover two clean-cut young men dressed in white shirts and dark three-piece suits. They inform you that they are members of The Church of Jesus Christ of Latter-day Saints, the Mormons. Your mind races. What do you say?

You respond, "We are Baptists; we believe in Jesus Christ."

They reply, "So do we. We are Christians who believe in Jesus also."

Confused, you catch yourself saying, "But I thought you guys were a cult. . . ."

Assignment: Using only your Bible, answer the following questions or propositions:
1. How do we know the Bible is complete?
2. How do we know God's truth has not been lost?
3. Prove Jesus is God.
4. Prove there is only one God.
5. Prove Jesus isn't the brother of Satan.
6. Prove we did not live in a spiritual preexistence being good and bad spirit children.
7. Prove God does not have a body.
8. Show why we do not baptize for the dead.

The initial reaction of most people is, some of these points are so ridiculous, why even bother with them. But there are people today in the United States who believe these things with all their hearts. The preceding concepts are part of Mormon (i.e., The Church of Jesus Christ of Latter-day Saints) doctrine. They believe that the Bible is incomplete; that the truth of God has been lost and restored through them; that Jesus is Deity but not the same God as God the Father; that there are more gods than just the ruling God of our earth; that Jesus is the brother of Satan; that we did live in a preexistence; that God has a body and, finally, that it is necessary to baptize for the dead.

The Mormons are not the only group with unique doctrines. Beginning in the 1800s, a new type of religion began appearing in "Christendom." Unlike the different groups already in existence that claimed to be orthodox and "right," these new groups took a step in a different direction. Most of the discussion in church history had centered around the doctrines of the Bible as the only Word of God and salvation as a product of works or grace or both. The new groups attacked an area that had not been touched since the early days of the Church Age (although they also maintained the controversy over salvation and the Bible). This new area of attack was against the Persons of God and Jesus Christ.

It was not a direct attack but very subtle, for it came from people who claimed, on the surface, to believe in Jesus Christ and God. Many of them were very sincere. In 1820, Joseph Smith and Mormonism appeared on the scene. In 1875, Mary Baker Eddy planted seeds that grew into the Christian Science movement. Also, we dare not forget Charles Taze Russell, who in 1879 started his Zion's Watchtower and Herald of Christ's Presence. This group became the Jehovah's Witnesses. The 1900s saw the rise of many more groups that questioned the Persons of God and Jesus Christ.

The Bible foretold that this would happen: "Then if any man shall say unto you, Lo, here is Christ, or there; believe it not. For there shall arise false Christs, and false prophets, and shall shew great signs and wonders; insomuch that, if it were possible, they shall deceive the very elect" (Matt. 24:23, 24). "Now the Spirit speaketh expressly, that in the latter times some shall depart from the faith, giving heed to seducing spirits, and doctrines of devils" (1 Tim. 4:1).

As frightening as it is to see the rise of the "Christian" cults around us, there is a promise in the midst of it all. When we as Biblically born-again believers see these things happen, we know that the coming of Christ is soon. We need to reach the dear people caught in the trap of a false god and false Christ with the message of the one true God and the Biblical Christ. This is what this book is all about. An important point to remember is this: It is not enough to know what you believe or why you believe it. You must know how to communicate it, for without real communication witnessing is a waste.

This book is designed to help you witness to religious people of all types. Many of the experiences and examples will deal with Mormonism, for I have been learning how to share Christ with these people for almost ten years. Even so, once an individual has learned to witness to one of these groups, he can witness to all of them. The principles used in witnessing are interchangeable, remaining basically the same. This book is based on lectures I have given as I spoke in churches aross the country. There have been many requests to put what I have shared in writing. The result is before you. May the Lord accomplish His purpose through these pages.

One final point: This book is not intended to be an exhaustive theological study of the doctrines it discusses. Instead we will zero in on exact verses and explain what they actually say so that real communication will result. When a person is involved in a discussion with a Mormon, he doesn't have time to explain a whole system of theology. He needs tangible reasons found in the Bible for what he believes. Now with this understood, let's get started.

One

Attitudes

A person's attitude often affects what he thinks of others and what they think of him. In the area of witnessing, and especially when witnessing to someone who holds a strong religious conviction, a person's attitude can determine whether a conversation will end on friendly or unfriendly terms. An argument can greatly damage the cause of Christ, and it may take years of work to repair that damage.

We must realize that people usually do not change their positions in just one discussion, especially if those positions have been held for years and believed in with all their hearts. Secondly, and most important, we don't change people; the Holy Spirit does. **The real burden of reaching these people for Christ rests with God.** We do not prove God is right; we merely share what is right. Truth is truth no matter what. When we cannot lead someone to the truth, we must realize that we have not failed; the one who does not accept the truth has failed.

Truth does not rise or fall depending on our words.

God's truth will still remain intact even if we do not "convince" the one who is wrong of what is right.

It is generally thought that it takes about five years to lead a Mormon to the Biblical Christ. That means there will be twenty to thirty Christians witnessing to him along the way. It's easy to be the thirtieth, the one who leads the individual to the Lord. It's tough to be the fourth or the sixteenth or twenty-second person and not see the results. Most of us will not see the results in this kind of witnessing; yet we cannot grow discouraged.

The easiest thing to do in a discussion with a Mormon is to charge in and "prove you are not a coward." It takes real courage to remain silent and polite when someone else twists your words or changes his position in mid-stream. There is a concept today which dictates that when a person of the cults comes to your door you are to draw your sword, attack, slice to pieces, and then put together a Christian from the pieces. **This is not a Biblical concept, so do not use it.** Leaving the discussion on friendly terms is more important than saying everything you want to say and departing as enemies. If you have used the "attack" method and regret it, remember what Paul said in Philippians 3:13 about "forgetting those things which are behind," and start out fresh with a new approach. There is a beautiful promise found in Romans 8:28 that God can take everything, including our mistakes, and work them for good. Leave the past with Him.

In order to witness to people who are in error regarding what God has said, two important areas must be fully functional within the person witnessing. The first is the love of God and the second is a knowledge of the Bible. One without the other will be ineffective. A person may have a knowledge of the Bible but lack love, and he will only succeed in driving people away. Another may have love but lack a knowledge of the Bible, so that not only will he be unable to share the truth, he may even become confused as to what the truth is.

Love

In John 13:34 we read the words of Christ: "A new commandment I give unto you, That ye love one another; as I have loved you, that ye also love one another." In a very real sense Christians have forgotten how to love. We must understand that love is the key to reaching people for Christ. Paul wrote in 2 Corinthians 5:14 that ". . . the love of Christ constraineth us. . . ." People wonder at the cults and their apparent zeal in spreading their faith. What is often forgotten is that cult members witness to other people because they believe that witnessing is one of the works they must do to get to Heaven. Christians believe that true salvation is accomplished by Christ alone apart from their works (Eph. 2:8, 9). Therefore, if we share the message of Christ it is not because we have to, but because we want to. We do it because of love.

In John 13:35 Jesus states: "By this shall all men know that ye are my disciples, if ye have love one to another." The world will know you are a disciple of Christ not because you go to church, or because you have been baptized or because you live a "good, clean Christian life." Why not? Certainly these things are important. When one goes to church, he is in a systematic study program of God's Word and enjoys fellowship with other believers. When one is baptized, he is following the Biblical way of publicly identifying himself with Christ. When one lives a moral life, he is protecting himself and his Christian testimony. Yet, Jesus said it would be their love that would let the world know. Why? The answer is because there is a whole religious world full of people out there who go to church, who are baptized, and who lead moral lives. There has to be something different and that something different is our love.

I knocked on a door in Utah and a Mormon lady answered. I told her I was from the local Baptist church, and she informed me she was going to slam the door in my face. When I inquired why, she told me that when her son had been on his mission, a Baptist had slammed the door in *his* face. Please don't slam the door in their faces. Have an attitude of love. If you do not know what to say when they come, explain that you cannot talk now and ask for their phone number so you can call them later. When they leave, call your pastor for advice, and then study!

Some people have a "two tract rack" attitude. We have one type of tract for people like the milkman or the mailman, with titles like "What must I do to be saved?" or "God loves you!" Then we have the other tract rack for the cults. The titles in this tract rack are "Why was Joseph Smith a false prophet?" or "Why Jehovah's Witnesses are not witnesses of Jehovah!" or "Why was Mary Baker Eddy off her rocker?"

Picture this situation: A couple of Mormon missionaries arrive at your door. You greet each other and then you hand them the tract, "Why was Joseph Smith a false prophet?" You know they're excited about receiving it. From now on they'll listen to everything you have to say, right? Wrong! You've lost them. So find good tracts that give the way of salvation and define the terms they use. The problem I have with many tracts is that the writers seem to think everyone in the world knows what the word "saved" means. Find a tract that explains what salvation is and how to receive it. **Do not give a tract that criticizes a person's religion or the founder of that religion.** Present the positive aspect of the Bible and what it teaches.

A Knowledge of the Bible

A knowledge of what the Bible teaches is crucial. In 1 Peter 3:15 we are told to ". . . be ready always to give an answer to every man that asketh you a reason of the hope that is in you. . . ." There is the challenge. It will be hard work to set aside time for concentrated Bible study, especially if you work a forty-hour-a-week job, but it is worth it. Since God has taken the time to tell us about Himself in the Bible, let us not content ourselves with settling for a second opinion.

Finally, we must realize that in dealing with the cults we are going to come across some strange concepts, ideas and stories. The standard by which we are to judge them is not because they are strange, but because their position contradicts the Bible.

Two

The Discussion

Part 1

What do you do when a Mormon, a Jehovah's Witness, or any other person belonging to a cult comes to your door? What do you say? "Ah—hello. I can't talk now, but our pastor lives down the street, the third house on the right. He'd better chance of converting you than I."

The answer to "What do you say?" is what the next two chapters are all about. It is important that we know how to respond in this kind of situation. What you are about to read is by no means an exact procedure, but a basic outline to follow and adapt to each situation.

What about 2 John 9, 10?

Before we go any further we need to face the discussion centered around 2 John 9, 10 which deals with allowing a conversation to occur in your home with a member of the cults. The verses read: "Whosoever transgresseth, and abideth not in the doctrine of Christ, hath not God. He that abideth in the doctrine of Christ, he hath both the Father and the Son. If there come any unto you, and bring not this doctrine, receive him not into your house, neither bid him God speed."

First, we need to recognize that there are good men on both sides of the issue concerning whether we should let a member of the cults into our homes. Whatever you believe these verses mean, they give no one the excuse not to witness to the cults. So whether you believe you can let them in your house or whether you believe they must remain at the door, you must still share Christ with them. It is important to use common sense. If you are a new Christian or one who is unsure of what to say or what you believe, put off the conversation until you have had time to study and prepare. (It may take years to prepare yourself, but keep working at it.) You might also want to consider setting up an appointment with them and sending the children to Grandma's for the evening.

Now, back to 2 John 9, 10. There are several ways to understand this passage without implying you cannot witness to cult members in your home. First, there are those who believe 2 John was written to a local church and sister churches it had started (i.e., ". . . the elect lady and her children . . ." in verse 1). If this is so, John was saying not to allow false teachers in the house of God or have them conduct church services. Therefore, the verse would not apply to your personal home. However, whether by interpretation or application, we should not allow false teachers to come into our home to instruct us. This does not mean we cannot allow them to come into our home with the purpose of witnessing to them.

I hold the following position based on the fact that there were all kinds of traveling teachers in the days of John the Apostle. Some were good and some were bad. John was saying not to give the bad ones a place to stay overnight and encourage them in their work (bid him Godspeed). This is not to be understood that we are not to help those in physical need who do not agree with us. We can help all men if we do it with the purpose of reaching them for Jesus Christ.

Opening Comments

An important fact to remember when the cult members approach you in your home is that it is *your* home and *you* can control the situation. Don't let any self-assured manner fool you. They know they are guests and ultimately they must respect your wishes.

When a Mormon or other cult member comes to your door you might begin the conversation like this: "I appreciate your coming by and wanting to share with me what you believe. There is nothing I enjoy more than discussing the Bible and what it has to say. I would like to share something with you first, if I may. I've seen some Bible discussions turn into debates and arguments. Neither person listened to the other because the person who was supposed to be listening was thinking about what he was going to say next. I don't want a debate. What I do enjoy is a discussion based on the priority of truth. You see, I want to know the truth of God above everything else. I want to know it above being a Baptist or a Mormon or any other religious person. That means if you share something with me I've never seen before, I promise you I'll study it this week, and then we can get together and discuss it again. At the same time, if I should show you something you have never seen before, you promise me you will study it this week, then we will discuss it when we get back together."

It is impossible under normal circumstances to say what you just read word for word; and, besides, that would be unnatural. What you want to do is get the basic idea of what you just read. There are three concepts:
1. **Seek the truth together**

2. **No debate**
3. **A week to review**

The week to review is important, for it takes the pressure off both of you and also challenges the other person to take time and study what you have shared. Remember, rarely are these people reached in one session. If at any time during the discussion you sense tempers rising, be honest and share the fact that you sense that pressure. Tell those you are talking to that you love them and want to discuss these things in love. (Be wise in this. A husband and wife together sharing Christ is quite effective. Having someone with you in any case is always a help and encouragement when you witness.)

We will follow a three-point outline in this discussion:
1. **Establish authority**
2. **Define terms**
3. **Zero in on salvation**

If I were to give a test at the end of these next two chapters, I would ask you to list these three areas. Of course, the real test is when some members of a cult sit down in your living room and you must meet the challenge of sharing Christ with them.

Establish Authority

The authority to determine right and wrong is very important. When one is tried in a courtroom, there must be laws to determine whether what that person did is right or wrong. When witnessing to cult members, since we are dealing with what God has said, it is important that a final authority be set up between the two parties to settle any dispute. No discussion is profitable if conclusions are reached based upon opinions. The important point is what God has said about the subject under discussion.

For the Biblical Christian the only authority that can be accepted is the Bible, but in the world of cults there are many authorities besides the Bible. One of the most common reasons cults give for the right of their existence is that the Bible has errors, or at least cannot be understood without help. The cults claim they are the ones who help correct the errors and help others understand. Mormons, for instance, have many authorities. They have the *Book of Mormon*, the *Pearl of Great Price*, the *Doctrine and Covenants*, the Bible (as far as it is, in their opinion, translated correctly), "a living prophet," twelve apostles, what they call the priesthood and, finally, they believe they themselves are receiving revelation. Since the Book of Mormon, Doctrine and Covenants and Pearl of Great Price are all written in a very similar style to the King James Version of the Bible, a Mormon can fire verses at you that prove his position until you ask him for the reference. Then you discover that the "verses" are from 2 Nephi or the Book of Abraham. Mormons are not the only ones who use authority other than the Bible, but they are certainly among the most outspoken about it. Many of the other groups hide behind the idea that they have the "correct interpretation" of the Bible.

In 2 Timothy 3:15, 16 we read, "And that from a child thou hast known the holy scriptures, which are able to make thee wise unto salvation through faith which is in Christ Jesus. All scripture is given by inspiration of God, and is profitable for doctrine, for reproof, for correction, for instruction in righteousness. . . ." I will not take space at this time to give the Biblical reasons for accepting the Bible and the Bible alone as our authority. There is a whole section in this book devoted to that purpose. But we can demonstrate how to make it the sole authority in a particular conversation.

Bible Cult

The words "Bible Cult" conjure up a paradox in the Biblical Christian's mind. We refer to those groups which accept the Bible in some form, but believe doctrine contradictory to the fundamental concepts of Biblical Christianity. Because these groups believe in the Bible (although they may have an incorrect view of it), the person sharing Christ with them has a starting point whereby he can establish the sole authority of the Bible.

We must realize in witnessing to these people of the cults that they are human and as nervous as we are. The difference is they talk more often about what they believe than the average Biblical Christian. Also, many cultists have a handbook or memorized procedure they have been taught to follow. This is especially true of the Mormons, so we will use them as an example of how to establish the Bible as the only authority in a conversation.

When the doorbell rings and you open the door, you discover two nice-looking, well-dressed young men who have parked their bicycles in your driveway. After using the procedure given in the "opening comments" section of this chapter (page 23), you are now ready to begin your discussion. The Mormon missionaries will begin to tell you a story. The story is about a young boy named Joseph Smith who, through his supposed vision of God and Jesus Christ, was to have restored the truth of God to the earth, truth which they believe had been lost. In other words, they believe Joseph Smith was a latter-day prophet and that, therefore, prophets exist today. Don't expect Mormons to begin discussing some of their "far-out" beliefs right away. The principle they follow is to get you to believe Joseph Smith is a prophet of God; then everything else he taught has to be right. When the Mormon comes to the part about Joseph Smith's vision, this is what, in essence, you say:

"Excuse me, but I'd like to share something with you that I believe will help us in discussing what the truth of God is. This is the United States of America, and you have the right to believe Joseph Smith is a prophet of God and that the Book of Mormon is Scripture along with the

Bible; but I must be honest with you, and I think you want me to be. Although you believe in Joseph Smith and the Book of Mormon, I do not. Now, this should not take you by surprise. After all, that is why you are here—to convince me the Book of Mormon is true and that Joseph Smith is a prophet of God. Since I do not believe either (and I don't mean that to sound hateful, just honest), you could quote to me Joseph Smith and the Book of Mormon all day, and it just would not mean a thing. The only authority I accept is the Bible. If you hope to show me your position is true, you must do so from the Bible."

Several things are happening at this point. First, you are not being unfair; you are being honest. You are asking the Mormon missionary to do with you what you would have to do with a Jewish individual who rejected the New Testament and accepted the Old. Secondly, you've set before him a proposition encouraging him to truly study the Bible in an attempt to find what he believes in it. **The first major step in leading a Mormon to the Biblical Christ is getting him to study the Bible.** What is his reaction to all this? I've yet to see a Mormon who will not take the challenge. If he does seem hesitant, ask him in love why he is frightened. If you are careful, this approach really works. I remember one occasion when I was talking with a Mormon missionary when he referred to the Pearl of Great Price to attempt to prove a point. Suddenly, he remembered the fact that I did not accept the Pearl of Great Price as Scripture and apologized.

One very important thing to remember at this point: **Don't ever begin to think of these people as "pushovers."** Many of them are proficient in presenting what they believe. Your task is not to convince them of your position, but to share in love the Biblical Christ.

In review: The purpose of establishing authority with a cult organization that claims at least a partial belief in the Bible is twofold. You do not have to use the exact method we have used here, but you should present these two positions in the form of a loving challenge:

1. Does the Bible allow for the cult's claim to divine authority, such as Joseph Smith's claim to being a prophet? (This does not involve attacking Joseph Smith or their belief's integrity. Instead you challenge them to discover if the Bible allows authority outside itself.)

2. Are the cults able to present their position from the Bible alone?

The Book of Mormon

There is a philosophy today which teaches that one way to witness to Mormons is to use the Book of Mormon references that contradict the Mormon position. Despite what Mormons might claim, the Book of Mormon does not teach Mormon doctrine. It basically teaches Bible doctrine with baptismal regeneration thrown in. The Book of Mormon was written in the early days of Mormonism before the rest of the doctrines were developed. Because of this, there are certain verses in the Book of Mormon which can be used to demonstrate that Mormonism is false. Examples are:

Alma 18:26-28: God is Spirit
Mosiah 15:1, 2, 5: Jesus is God
Moroni 8:18: God does not change

The problem is this: Once you use the Book of Mormon as an authority, you give the Mormon you are talking to the right to use it, and he knows it better than you do. Besides, if you do not believe it is Scripture, what it says makes no difference.

The New World Translation

Jehovah's Witnesses present a unique problem of their own. They have rewritten the Bible in what they call *The New World Translation*. (The Reorganized Church of Jesus Christ of Latter Day Saints has done the same thing in their *Inspired Version of the Bible.*) The Jehovah's Witnesses claim that great Bible scholars were involved in the translation, but no list is provided for examination (at least at the time of this writing).

What do you do when you meet someone who belongs to a cult that has rewritten the Bible? First, be honest. Tell them you don't accept their translation. Make sure you say it in an attitude of love. Through the rest of the conversation, share Bible verses which teach the Biblical way of salvation. You will find, in some cases, that they are almost the same in the false version. Where your version and their version disagree, attempt to demonstrate the true position. If you know Hebrew or Greek, it will help. But since most people do not, the use of the other good translations may prove helpful. Patience and love are the keys.

Non-Bible Cult

There are other types of religious cults in existence today, the origins of which began in the Far Eastern religions and philosophies. What do you do when you meet someone who does not accept the Bible as an authority at all? First, and this is quite important, never apologize for believing the Bible to be the Word of God. Next, find a common ground upon which to approach the discussion. Paul did this in his Mars Hill sermon when he said: "Ye men of Athens, I perceive that in all things ye are too superstitious. For as I passed by, and beheld your devotions, I found an altar with this inscription, TO THE UNKNOWN GOD. Whom therefore ye ignorantly worship, him declare I unto you. God that made the world and all things therein, seeing that he is Lord of heaven and earth, dwelleth not in temples made with hands; Neither is worshipped with men's hands, as though he needed any thing, seeing he giveth to all life, and breath, and all things; And hath made of one blood all nations of men for to dwell on all the face of the earth, and hath determined the times before appointed, and the bounds of their habitation; That they should seek the Lord, if haply they might feel after him, and find him, though he be not far from every one of us: For in him we live, and move, and have our being; as certain also of your own poets have said, For we are also his offspring. Forasmuch then as we are the offspring of God, we ought not to think that the Godhead is like unto gold, or silver, or stone, graven by art and man's device. And the times of this ignorance God winked at; but now commandeth all men every where to repent: Because he hath appointed a day, in the which he will judge the world in righteousness by that man whom he hath ordained; whereof he hath given assurance unto all men, in that he hath raised him from the dead" (Acts 17:22-31).

Paul shared the fact with these people that God was personal and knowable. There are three key areas we can derive from this fact:

1. **God has spoken** (Heb. 1:1, 2). Share with the individual that God has truly communicated with us in human language. We can know His will. The obvious question is, "What did He say?" This opens the door for use of the Bible.

2. **God has come to us** (1 Tim. 3:16). The important message of Biblical Christianity is the fact that God has done the work for us. He made the effort to reach man. This sets Biblical Christianity apart from the religious world which is making the effort to reach God.

3. **Person of Christ** (Acts 8:35). We need to take the same approach with these people that Philip did with the Ethiopian eunuch. We must present the Person of Christ. Introduce these people to the Savior and share what He has done for them and how they may receive His gift of eternal life.

Three

The Discussion

Part 2

Define Terms

Communication is the most important factor in reaching the people of the cults with the Biblical Christ. If you do not communicate what you want to say, you are wasting your time. I cannot number the times that I have shared Christ with Mormons and have had them say, "I've talked with a lot of Baptists before, but you're the first one who was able to explain to me what you believe." This does not mean that these Baptists did not know what they believed or the Biblical reasons for believing it. It does mean they had great difficulty in expressing their beliefs so the Mormon could understand what was being said. Think of how many times you've been in a witnessing situation and the person you were speaking to agreed with everything you said; yet you knew his beliefs weren't the same as yours.

Let us examine Mormonism for a moment. Mormonism is very much an "end justifies the means" religion. This sounds harsh, but I do not make this statement with any malice. I make it based on various conversations I have had with Mormons. In most cases it is not a direct attempt at deception, but a simple withholding of all the facts until you have made your commitment to the Mormon belief that Joseph Smith was a prophet of God.

One area in which deception is quite commonly used is in their unique belief about the Godhead. Mormons believe in what they call *exaltation*. This is the belief that God was once a man (probably the Savior) of a previous earth. He did what he was supposed to do and therefore became the ruling god of this earth. That God's god was a man on an earth that existed previous to God's earth, did what he was supposed to do and became the ruling god for *his* earth. Each man on our earth has the opportunity of going on and ruling his own earth if he is obedient to the Mormon gospel. In fact, there is a basic belief that the whole universe is filled with gods producing men who become gods who produce men. This process is going on from eternity past to eternity future. Mormons have a saying, "As man is, God once was. As God is, man may become." Joseph Smith stated, ". . . you have got to learn how to be gods yourselves . . ." All of the above is described in Bruce R. McConkie's (a Mormon) *Mormon Doctrine*, pages 169, 240, 256-258, 321, 323, 576, 577.

Although these facts are believed by the informed Mormon, if they were presented to him he might reply, "That is not Mormon doctrine." But if he were asked if these things were true Mormon *concepts*, his reply, if he were pinpointed, would be "yes." You may be asking yourself how he could honestly do that. The answer is simple in the Mormon's mind. Mormon doctrine is that which appears in the standard works, that is, the Book of Mormon, Doctrine and Covenants, the Pearl of Great

Price, and the Bible ("as far as it is translated correctly"). Any other concepts held by the Mormon church are not official doctrines, although they are believed in with all their hearts. This, despite the fact that these other concepts appear as doctrine in Bruce McConkie's *Mormon Doctrine*. One point we might add in all fairness: There are Mormons who do not hide behind this line of reasoning, but openly admit this "gods producing men who become gods" as doctrine. Others will usually admit that the standard works teach the plurality of gods, but these are mysteries, and we do not need to concern ourselves with them.

The reason we took so much space on this point is to make the reader aware of the importance of defining what he believes and not taking at face value what he hears. We must remember that the cults use the same terms we use, but they have redefined those terms in their system of theology. I will illustrate this by giving my testimony as if I were a Mormon.

Mormon testimony: "I have received Jesus Christ as my Savior. I have faith in Christ. I believe in Him. I have been saved by God's grace through Christ's shed blood, and I know I am going to Heaven when I die. I have been born again."

What you have just read probably sounded like Biblical doctrine. Most people coming for membership in a local church would be quite welcomed with the testimony just given. Not every Mormon will be this deceptive in what he believes, but there are some who are quite proficient at it. We must also remember that this terminology problem is not necessarily a deliberate deception. It stems, as we have already mentioned, from the fact that the cults have taken Biblical terms and given them new definitions. They can say these terms without intentionally lying. Now, let us get back to that Mormon testimony. What did he really mean when he gave it?

Explanation of Mormon testimony:

1. Received Christ—Received the Church of Jesus Christ of Latter-day Saints. Became a Mormon.

2. Has faith in Christ—To believe or have faith is the first step in a long series of steps that are necessary if one hopes to be with God some day. Faith is also thought of in another way. When a Mormon says he has faith, he can mean he has the right faith. In other words, he is of the Mormon faith.

3. Saved by grace through Christ's shed blood—This is not special to the Mormon, for he believes that everyone on the entire earth will be saved by God's grace through Christ's shed blood; but that does not mean, according to the Mormon, that everyone will be with God. The salvation he is speaking of is the resurrection of mankind. Everyone will be resurrected, but not everyone will be with God.

4. Knows he is going to Heaven—Mormons believe in three kingdoms or heavens, but God only dwells in the highest Heaven. Everybody on earth is going to one of these kingdoms. Where one goes is determined by how worthy one is in this life. Therefore, a Mormon knows he will be in heaven when he dies; he just does not know which one.

5. Born again—this means baptism to the Mormon.

When we talk with people from the cults, we must be in the practice of defining our terms throughout the entire conversation. As I wrote earlier, the biggest problem I find with most tracts is the careless way their writers use Biblical terms, expecting everyone to know what they mean. This mistake is easily made in a witnessing conversation, also. Do not take it for granted that the people you are talking to understand what you are saying. Often they do not, and until they do, nothing can be accomplished. This process of establishing communication can take hours. I have seldom talked with a Mormon for less than an hour.

I remember an incident which took place at the Bible college I attended. A couple of fellows with bald heads wearing white robes and sandals walked on campus wanting something to eat and drink. Some of the students assisted them in this. As they were leaving, another student and I asked if we could talk to them. They told us they had an eternity of time (or something to that effect). We all four sat down on the grass, each of us looking for ants. (In Florida one does not sit down on the grass without looking for ants.) We were not very far along in the conversation before we realized why they did not want to sit on the ants. It was not for fear of being bitten, but they believed the ants were their brothers, and they did not want to harm them. At this point in the conversation, it was very important that we remembered that these people were wrong, not because of a strange belief but because they disagreed with the Bible.

The conversation seemed to go on for hours without the feeling of accomplishing anything. They would share with me doctrine totally contrary to everything I understood the Bible to teach, but when I shared in return the truths of God's Word, they would nod their heads in agreement. I was at the point of screaming inside, and several times came very close to giving up. Nevertheless, they were quite willing to continue the conversation, so we remained. It seemed as if it took forever, but finally I expressed a certain Biblical truth in a carefully worded phrase. For the first time since we started, they admitted they didn't believe what I had said. It still took awhile, but that was the breakthrough. Ultimately, we were able to share Christ with them so that, for the first time in their lives, they understood Who He really is and His way to God. They decided it was time to leave.

When we witness to these people we must realize we do not reach them in a ten-minute visit. We have got to be willing to give time—hours of our lives if necessary—to reach these people for Christ. Because of this terminology problem and the limits of any one human mind, it is impossible to be totally prepared in knowing every doctrine of every cult and what the perfect response is at any given moment. Therefore, many people are afraid to witness to the cults. We cannot carry this burden when we witness to these people. We must remember that the Holy Spirit is the One Who will lead them to Christ. We can be as ready as possible, though, and that requires determination on our part.

In order to define terms, we must know the Biblical definitions of these terms. Do you believe what you believe because you have found it in the Bible, or do you believe it because your pastor has said it is in the Bible? Take time to sit down and write out Biblical definitions, and their Scripture references, for the terms you use. Let us examine a Biblical word that is often used without very much thought—the familiar word "saved."

Saved

1. Dictionary definition: to be delivered from danger or peril.

2. Biblical definition: We are delivered from God's wrath through a personal trust in Christ (Rom. 5:9; John 3:36; 1 Thess. 1:10).

3. Question: What is the wrath of God? Answer: Biblical hell (Rev. 14:10).

There certainly is more to the Biblical fact of salvation than just listed, but what we shared would be a good start in understanding the word "saved."

Use Terms That Work

Not only do we need to define terms, but we need to use only those Biblical expressions that will clarify what we are trying to say to the cult members. Often we discover these expressions by trial and error, learning during an actual conversation what works best for that particular person. A couple of examples can be given here to illustrate what I mean. For instance, in witnessing to a Mormon do not say, "I know I will be in Heaven when I die." A Mormon believes he knows this also, for there are three possible heavens he may go to. According to Mormon theology, God only lives in the highest Heaven, Therefore, when you witness to a Mormon, tell him you know you will be with God, the Father, when you die. The Scripture verse backing this position is John 14:6. If you are witnessing to a Jehovah's Witness, you will get his attention quickly by saying you know you will be with Jehovah when you die. He does not really believe he has much of a chance for that, but it is the highest possible "reward" he is trying for.

When witnessing to a Mormon, do not just carelessly say "The Scriptures teach this . . ." (in reference to a certain position you hold). Remember, the Mormons have many scriptures. You would do well to say, "This is what God's Word, the Bible, teaches."

Zero in on Salvation

Of all the subjects available to discuss during the conversation with a person from a cult, the most important is the subject of salvation. Ultimately, nothing else really matters. The proper awareness of God's true salvation is crucial to where we will spend eternity. For instance, if a Mormon comes to your door, do not get into a discussion on polygamy. The Mormon church officially condemns the practice of polygamy today, but there are still Mormons in the mountains of Utah who practice it. It is not difficult to prove polygamy is wrong, for 1 Timothy 3:2, 12 and Titus 1:6 teach the one-wife principle. It is conceivable to prove to a Mormon polygamy is wrong and have him leave your house still lost and going to hell. We must get our priorities straight.

There are three very important areas worth discussing under the topic of salvation. All three of these fall naturally into place after the establishment of the Bible as your authority. These three areas are:

1. The Person of the Savior—It is worth taking time to show Who Jesus is. This involves the very important fact that Jesus is God. Many people fail to grasp this great necessity to our salvation. If Jesus is not God (Who by nature is an infinite being), it would have been impossible to pay the eternal punishment for sin in a set period of time on the cross.

2. The work of the Savior—It is worth taking time to show what Christ accomplished on the cross. John 3:14-16 and Romans 5:6-10 teach that Christ was shedding His blood to satisfy God's righteous anger toward sin. Hebrews 9:22 teaches there must be shedding of blood before forgiveness of sins can take place, and Hebrews 10:10-14 teaches that Christ suffered only one time for our sins. (This differs from the Roman Catholic view that He suffers over and over during Holy Communion.) Finally, Romans 3:24, 25 teach that it is faith in Christ's shed blood that appropriates God's forgiveness of our sins. (See also Acts 10:43.) Nothing else! This is what God says, despite the claim by the Mormons that a personal belief in Christ's shed blood for salvation is just our opinion. (See *What the Mormons Think of Christ*, p. 31, first paragraph under "The blood of Christ" section. This is a Mormon publication that is given away free at any Mormon visitor center.)

3. The grace of God—Think of the excitement that would spread through true Christianity if we all could grasp the full realization of the uniqueness of God's salvation and His amazing grace. Think of the

thrill we can experience when we see in the eyes of a member of a cult the light of understanding, for the first time, of this great truth. In a world of religion where people are trying to work their way to God, we bring the wonderful news that God has worked His way to man in the Person of Christ. The struggle to be right with God is over when we trust Christ by God's undeserved favor to make us right with God.

What Actually Saves Us?

There is a trap often used by the cults to confuse many Christians as to what actually saves them. What does save us? Does our believing save us? One day you may find yourself in the following situation with a cult member. You have just shared with him the fact that you do nothing for your salvation—that Jesus has done it all. He smiles and makes this reply, "Oh, yes, you do. You have to ask Jesus to save you. We believe we have to do that also, but we do not stop there. We add to that many other things. There is no difference between us, though. You do one work—believe. We do that and more. You do one work; we do many. But we are both working."

This kind of thinking is quite logical if you fall into the trap that believing is a work. This is a dangerous concept for it is quite anti-Biblical. Think this through. When you trusted in Christ, did that earn the merit of Christ in your salvation? Did God give you so many points in Heaven? No! Remember, **one of the certain signs of a false religion is that a person must do something to earn the merit of Christ.** Does our trusting save us? Again, the answer is no! It is Christ Who saves us. Trusting is merely the channel through which that saving power of Christ comes. Let me illustrate. If my hands were dirty and I went to a sink to wash them, I would turn on the water faucet. But turning on the water faucet is not what cleanses my hands—the water cleanses my hands. Turn-

39

ing on the water faucet merely allows the water to clean my hands. So, too, our trusting in Christ allows Him to save us.

There are groups today that are making a major mistake; they believe their trusting saves them. With that logic, they have an "on again, off again" salvation; that is, they believe they can lose their salvation. Today they are trusting; tomorrow they may not. The Biblical fact is that Christ saves; therefore, we can never lose our salvation. Let us not make the mistake of trusting in our trusting. Let us do it the Biblical way. Let us trust in Christ alone to save us.

There may be someone reading this who is thinking about John 6:28, 29, which reads, "Then said they unto him, What shall we do, that we might work the works of God? Jesus answered and said unto them, This is the work of God, that ye believe on him whom he hath sent." The important thing to note is Jesus' reply. He stated that believing was the work of God, not a work of man.

There is one more important area under the point of salvation—the difference between believing and trusting. The following illustration applies both to salvation and to the daily life of a Christian. A world-famous tightrope walker announced he was going to put a tightrope across Niagara Falls and walk across it with a wheelbarrow. People showed up by the thousands, and he actually did this feat several times. Finally, one person in the crowd grew so excited he jumped up and said to the tightrope walker, "I believe you are the best tightrope walker in the world; I believe you could walk back and forth with that wheelbarrow a thousand times and never fall."

The tightrope walker replied, "Do you really believe that?"

The excited observer responded, "Yes, I believe that with all my heart!"

The tightrope walker smiled and said, "Then get in the wheelbarrow."

The observed remained an observer.

When it comes to salvation, **it is not enough to believe Jesus can save us.** We must trust Him to do so. When it comes to our Christian life, it is not enough to believe that God will take care of us. We must trust Him to do so.

Closing Comments

How one closes a conversation with cultists is just as important as how one opens it. There comes a time in each discussion when the parties sense it is drawing to a close. When you sense this, allow it to happen. Believe that the Holy Spirit is working. Of course it is always a joy to end the discussion by having the individual accept Christ; but, as we shared before, that is not always the way God works.

In the case of Mormons, you will know their side of the conversation is drawing to a close when they turn in the Book of Mormon to Moroni 10:4 and read, "And when ye shall receive these things, I would exhort you that ye would ask God, the Eternal Father, in the name of Christ, if these things are not true; and if ye shall ask with a sincere heart, with real intent, having faith in Christ, he will manifest the truth of it unto you, by the power of the Holy Ghost. . . ." Then the Mormon will say something to this effect: "I would like to share my testimony with you. I have done as this verse says and asked God if these things were true. He has shown me they are true. I know Joseph Smith was a prophet of God called to minister on the earth in these latter days. I know the Book of Mormon is true scripture just like the Bible, and I know that you can know this if you sincerely ask God. He will show you through the power of the Holy Ghost." Sounds impressive, doesn't it? Many people are brought into the Mormon church because of this challenge. Is it a valid request? I'd like to give you a few points to consider.

1. Examine Moroni 10:4 and think through the logic behind it. What it is really saying is this: If you will ask God if these things are true, believing they are true, He'll show you they are true. In other words, if you make up your mind before you ask, God will show you. An ancient philosopher once said, "We believe whatever we want to believe."

2. I took this challenge, before I knew better, when I first started studying Mormonism. The result was God showed me it was not true, but he showed me through a study of the Bible in relationship to Mormonism.

3. I can make just as strong a claim through the testimony of the Holy Spirit in my life; I know I'm right.

We don't remove the working of the Holy Spirit in our lives today. We believe the Holy Spirit is bearing witness with our spirit (Rom. 8:16); that He is teaching born-again Christians (1 John 2:27); that we cannot know God without Him (1 Cor. 2:14). Nevertheless, we must have an authority outside our personal experience to instruct us in what is right. The reason for this is obvious.

Lloyd Larkin, a missionary in Utah to the Mormons, gave this excellent illustration. Let us pretend to take ten people of ten different religions and line them up, among them a Mormon, Jehovah's Witness, Christian Scientist and Roman Catholic. Ask them to get down on their knees and ask God what the true church is. One . . . two . . . three. Down on their knees they go. Time is up. They stand.

"Mr. Mormon, what did God show you the true church is?"

"Why, God told me my church is the true church."

"Mr. Jehovah's Witness?"

"God showed me my church is the true church."

"Mr. Christian Scientist?"

"God showed me my church is the true church."

. . . And on down the line you go, getting the same results. There must be an authority outside ourselves to determine who is right. The Bible is that authority. After the Mormon has shared his testimony, one of the best Bible references to turn to is 1 John 5:9-13. This passage is a good closing passage for all cults. It is very important to leave them with something to think about until you have a chance to talk with them again. Let us examine together 1 John 5:9-13:

Verse 9—"If we receive the witness of men, the witness of God is greater: for this is the witness of God which he hath testified of his Son." It is more important to have the personal testimony of God concerning Jesus than the opinion of any man.

Verse 10—"He that believeth on the Son of God hath the witness in himself. . . ." We do not deny the testimony of the Holy Spirit in our lives; but as we are about to see, God's recorded Word is the more certain knowledge. ". . . He that believeth not God hath made him a liar; because he believeth not the record that God gave of his Son." What is God's true record?

Verses 11 and 12—"And this is the record, that God hath given to us eternal life, and this life is in his Son. He that hath the Son hath life; and he that hath not the Son of God hath not life." The truth is simply stated here. Works are completely removed. If you have Jesus, you have salvation. If you don't have Jesus, you don't have salvation. There is no in-between.

Verse 13—"These things have I written unto you that believe on the name of the Son of God; that ye may know that ye have eternal life, and that ye may believe on the name of the Son of God." The eternal life spoken of here cannot mean endless existence only; that everyone has endless existence and can know it. The context teaches that this eternal life comes through having the Son. Some will not have Him, therefore missing out on eternal life (1 John 5:12).

At this point in the discussion, it is very important that you zero in on the fact that a person can know he has eternal life. Here is an example of a conversation in which a Christian, Mr. Green, drives home this point to a Mormon missionary.

MR. GREEN: What we have read in 1 John 5:13, that we can know we have eternal life, is very real. Because of what God has said, I know I have eternal life. I know I will be with God when I die. Sir, do you know that you will be with God when you die?

MISSIONARY: *(Gives reply)*

(If he says he does not know for sure, point out that the Bible says he can know from 1 John 5:13. If he says he does know, and you will have some say it, ask the following question.)

MR. GREEN: May I ask you an important question?
MISSIONARY: Yes.
MR. GREEN: If I were to join your church, what is the minimum amount of things I must do in order to make it to God?

MISSIONARY: *(Gives reply)*

(If he cannot give you a list, then share with him he cannot really know he will make it to God because he does not know how much he must do. Remind him that God says you can know you have eternal life. If he does give you a list, help him with it. Ask him if church membership, baptism, communion, missionary work, good works and anything else you can think of are necessary. If he says any of these are not necessary, ask him if he will make it to God without doing the thing not necessary if it is within his power to do it. Help him to make the list as long as possible. Then ask the following question:)

MR. GREEN: Have you done everything on your list?
MISSIONARY: *(Gives reply)*

(If he has not done all the things on his list for salvation, then by his own standards he cannot know he has eternal life. In fact, he must be lost. Yet, God says you can know you will be with Him. If he says he has done everything on the list, ask him this last question:)

MR. GREEN: Can you guarantee me beyond all possible doubt that you will always continue to do everything on your list?

MISSIONARY: *(Gives reply)*

(If he is honest, he cannot make such a guarantee. When he admits this, remind him he cannot know he has eternal life if he can lose it, for eternal life by its very nature cannot be lost. It is eternal. First John 5:13 says we can *know*.)

It is a wonderful experience to lead the person you are talking with to the Lord at this point in the discussion. However, if you are unable to, end the conversation as a concerned friend, keeping the door open for yourself or the next person God brings into his life.

Outline of Discussion

I. Opening comments
  A. Seek the truth
  B. No debate
  C. A week to review

II. Discussion
  A. Establish authority (2 Tim. 3:15-17)
    1. Bible cult (2 Tim. 3:15-17)
      a. Bible is only authority
      b. Discussion must be limited to the Bible
    2. Non-Bible cult (Acts 17:22-31)
      a. God has spoken (Heb. 1:1, 2)
      b. God has come to us (1 Tim. 3:16)
      c. Person of Christ (Acts 8:35)
  B. Define terms
    1. Know meaning of Biblical terms
    2. Ask for definitions

3. Use terms that work
 C. Zero in on salvation (Acts 4:12)
   1. The Person of the Savior—He is God (Heb. 2:8)
   2. The work of the Savior—paid for personal sins (1 John 2:1, 2)
   3. The grace of God—salvation is by grace through faith (Eph. 2:8, 9)
III. Closing comments
 A. End in a friendly relationship
 B. Share the fact that we can know we have eternal life (1 John 5:13)

Four

Authority of the Bible

This section of the book is designed to help prepare serious students for a multitude of problems they may face in witnessing to cult members. It is impossible to cover every area, but the ones dealt with here are the most common. The outline form is designed to help facilitate the learning process and to make quick, easy reference to. Also, the subjects are listed alphabetically in each chapter.

Bible

Explanation: It is very important from a Biblical standpoint that we realize why the Bible is the only Word of God that God has given. There are many groups today who do not believe the Bible is complete. They may add to it in the form of additional "scripture" or lay claims to a living prophet among them. There are also claims that the Bible has become corrupt through the centuries, that a total apostasy from the truth has taken place. Therefore, according to them, they need to correct the Bible so we will have an accurate translation. What the Bible teaches about itself is one of the most important questions we can answer. In working with Mormons, there is a twofold approach which is quite effective. First, demonstrate the Bible is complete, and that we do not need additional revelation. If they insist on additional revelation, go to approach number two which is as follows: Even if revelation did exist today, it could not be on the basis that the truth of God was lost and needed to be restored. The outline gives the reasons why.

I. The Bible alone is our authority.
   A. It teaches everything we need to know about God (2 Tim. 3:15, 16).
      1. Teaches salvation through faith (v. 15).
      2. Teaches doctrine and how to be right with God (v. 16).
   B. Record of God is more certain than the testimony of men (1 John 5:9-11).
   C. Once Scripture came into being, it was more sure than a supposed vision from Heaven (2 Pet. 1:16-21). Paul warned against claims by people of angelic visitors from Heaven in Galatians 1:8, 9.

II. The Bible is without error.
   A. The Bible does not need to be corrected (Ps. 12:6, 7).
   B. The Bible or God's truth does not need to be restored because God's truth can never be lost. (There are verses in the Bible that speak of apostasy, but there are no verses that teach a total apostasy.)
      1. God's truth endures to all generations (Ps. 100:5).
      2. God's words will be in the mouths of his people always (Isa. 59:21).

3. The Word of God cannot become corrupt (1 Pet. 1:23).

III. The Bible is complete (we do not need additional Scripture).
   A. The Biblical faith was once for all delivered to the saints (Jude 3). It does not need to be restored over and over again.
   B. That which the apostles wrote would be the foundation of the Church Age (Eph. 2:19, 20). Just as Jesus would not remain in physical presence with us, neither would the apostles.
   C. The apostles' job was to complete the Word of God (Col. 1:25). "Fulfill" means to complete.
   D. By the death of the last apostle (John, as history records) we would have the "all truth" of God (John 14:26; 16:13). The night before He is to die, Jesus speaks to the disciples who are to be His apostles. He informs them that when the Spirit of truth comes, He will guide them into all truth. They will be the instruments used to complete God's recorded truth.
   E. The Bible states there were only twelve apostles (Rev. 21:14). Other people were called apostles (special messengers) but only twelve people were to hold that office. The Bible indicates that one of the requirements is that a person must see Christ personally to be an apostle. This would make Paul the replacement of Judas (1 Cor. 9:1). The groups today who claim to have living apostles contradict Scripture.
   F. With the coming of Christ, the age of the prophets was drawing to a close (Heb. 1:1, 2).
      1. There are those who try to take Amos 3:7 and use it to prove the need for prophets today. The verse reads, "Surely the Lord GOD will do nothing but he revealeth his secret unto

his servants the prophets." We do not deny God's use of men to reveal His truth (2 Pet. 1:21), but there came a time when God had revealed all that He wanted man to know.

2. Another claim is made for the need of prophets and apostles, using Ephesians 4:11-13. "And he gave some, apostles; and some, prophets; and some, evangelists; and some, pastors and teachers; For the perfecting of the saints, for the work of the ministry, for the edifying of the body of Christ: Till we all come in the unity of the faith, and of the knowledge of the Son of God, unto a perfect man, unto the measure of the stature of the fulness of Christ." The question is asked, "Have we come into the unity of faith?" In one sense we have. Verse fourteen tells us that when this unity of faith and knowledge comes, we will not be tossed about by every false doctrine that comes along. In other words, we will have the means to know the truth at our disposal. How is it we know true doctrine? The written Word of God is the answer (2 Tim. 3:16). Whatever "unity of faith" means, there is nothing in this passage that dictates the time length each of the offices given will last. Apostles and prophets were to give revelation while the evangelists, pastors and teachers were to instruct us in the revelation given. Each one does his part (Eph. 4:16). When the revelation was complete, apostles and prophets would cease to be. Evangelists, pastors and teachers would, by their very nature, continue. Also, if "unity of the faith" meant the second coming of Christ as some (usually Mormons) claim,

then the logical conclusion is there could be no total apostasy, for the divine offices of verse 11 (at least some of them) would have to continue until the coming of Christ. This also would destroy the Mormon position that these divine offices ceased to exist in their entirety and had to be restored.
G. We are told not to add or take away from God's Word (Rev. 22:18, 19). It was not by accident that God placed these words in the last part of the last book of the Bible. However, I would caution anyone about using this passage as a proof text that the Bible is complete, especially in dealing with the cults. Their reply will be that this is a particular warning given for the book of Revelation, and they are technically right. They will also point out there are two other times in Scripture when we are given just such a warning (Deut. 4:2 and Prov. 30:5, 6). Their question is this: "Do you stop Scripture being given at Deuteronomy or Proverbs? If not, what gives you the right to stop it at Revelation?" So remember, the Revelation passage does not contain the only verses that indicate the Bible is complete.

IV. The Bible and the Book of Mormon
A. There are various references in the Bible to prophets given books by God (Ezek. 2:9) or books seen in a vision (Isa. 29:4, 11-14). The Mormons claim that these verses are referring to the Book of Mormon. The answer rests in the context where the verses are found. In the majority of cases, the Old Testament verses used by the Mormons to prove their position deal directly with the nation of Israel, both in the immediate sense and prophetically. There is no

reason to single out the Book of Mormon as the prophetic fulfillment. Why not the Koran or other "scriptures" men have produced throughout history? One might even make the claim that the Old Testament is referring to the New. The best answer is that these references are illustrations God uses to present the point of the passage under question.

B. The two sticks in Ezekiel 37:15-20 are supposed to be, according to the Mormons, representatives of the Bible and the Book of Mormon, indicating that the two "scriptures" would eventually be one. Actually the next two verses (Ezek. 37:21, 22) teach the two sticks are, instead, the nations of Judah and Israel.

C. The Mormons say the phrase "other sheep" of John 10:16 applies to the Jewish people (House of Israel) they claim came to the American continent in the Book of Mormon story. But the context (John 9:13—10:39) actually teaches Christ was speaking to the House of Israel. He was informing them He had other sheep who were not of the House of Israel—not Jewish! Who? The Gentiles who would believe on Him!

Priesthood

Explanation: Priesthood is linked with authority not only in the cults, but also among other "Christian" religions. The authority of their priesthood gives them, within their doctrine, divine control of the Word of God and their followers. To counter their concepts, we must know what Biblical priesthood was and is all about.

The main issues are:
1. Is every believer a priest, or are there special offices today?
2. What is the difference between the Aaronic

priesthood and the Melchisedec priesthood?
I. The Aaronic priesthood
   A. They were of the tribe of Levi (Heb. 7:5). Any claim of the Aaronic priesthood must come from a Levi Jew.
   B. Their main responsibility was to intercede for the sins of the people of Israel by presenting the blood of slain animals within the veil of the temple (Heb. 9:6, 7). If a person claims to be an Aaronic priest, he must perform blood sacrifices.
   C. The Levi Aaronic priesthood had to be transferred from generation to generation because each generation had the natural habit of dying (Heb. 7:23).
II. The Melchisedec priesthood
   A. Jesus is the only Person to be made a Priest after the order of Melchisedec (Heb. 7:15-22). Anyone else making the claim cannot be Biblical.
   B. Jesus, our Melchisedec Priest, offered Himself as the blood Sacrifice (Heb. 9:11, 12). He replaced the Aaronic priests.
   C. Jesus will continue forever in His priesthood position—it will not be given to another (Heb. 7:24). The word "unchangeable" in the King James Version is "intransmissible" in the Greek.
III. The Christian priesthood
   A. When Christ died, the veil of the temple through which only the High Priest could enter the presence of God was torn in two (Matt. 27:51). This act signified that the way into God's presence was open to anyone who came to God through Jesus Christ (John 14:6). Since a priest was the only one who could enter in before, this made all believers priests.
   B. Peter taught that every believer holds a royal priesthood position (1 Pet. 2:5-9).

Five

The Nature of God

God

Explanation: There are several key areas concerning Who God is and what He is like that have come under attack by the cults. What does the Bible teach in these areas?

I. Only one God (Isa. 45:18, 22)
   A. The Mormons argue that the verses referring to only one God mean God is the only God we deal with, that there are others elsewhere in the universe. However, this argument ignores the literal, common-sense understanding of the verses. Mormons may use the following illustration to try to prove their position. God says in Exodus 20:13, "Thou shalt not kill," yet in Genesis 9:6 He gives an exception. God may state He is the only God, but in "other revelation" He gives the exception. This kind of

Mormon logic is misleading if not thought through carefully. Had God said, "Thou shalt not kill under any circumstances," then there could have been no exceptions; but He did not say that. In the area of God being the only God, He did in no uncertain terms say He was the only God. "Know therefore this day, and consider it in thine heart, that the LORD he is God in heaven above, and upon the earth beneath: there is none else" (Deut. 4:39). A question to ask a Mormon is this: "If God was indeed the only God in the entire universe and wanted you to know, how would He express it?" Just about any way the Mormon replies is used in the Bible.
  B. If there were other gods in the universe, certainly God would know about them, but He states He knows of no others (Isa. 44:8).
II. No one else can become a god. (Mormon doctrine teaches that the main purpose of our existence is to become a god.)
  A. The temptation to be like God was the downfall of Satan (Isa. 14:14).
  B. Satan used this lie in the Garden of Eden with Eve (Gen. 3:5).
  C. God said there could be no gods before or after Him (Isa. 43:10).
  D. Misunderstood verses
    1. John 10:34: "Jesus answered them, Is it not written in your law, I said, Ye are gods?" Jesus could not have meant that the religious hypocrites He was speaking to were gods. (The Mormons who use this verse ignore their theological teaching that we cannot become gods in this life, but only in the resurrection.) What did Jesus mean? First, He

quoted Psalm 82:6, and all of Psalm 82 deals with judgment. The people referred to in Psalm 82 had become as gods to Israel because of their position to judge Israel. The name for gods is *elohim,* meaning "strong ones." It is a term often used for God throughout the Old Testament. Hence its translation, "gods," in this verse. When it is used as a title for God, it is usually in the plural form, which emphasizes the multiple greatness of the one true God. Secondly, in John 10:30-39 Jesus is making a strong statement in regard to His deity. If God would call mere men gods, how much more appropriate for Christ to take the title Son of God since He was and is God the Son.

2. First Corinthians 8:5, 6: "For though there be that are called gods, whether in heaven or in earth, (as there be gods many, and lords many,) But to us there is but one God, the Father, of whom are all things, and we in him; and one Lord Jesus Christ, by whom are all things, and we by him." The context teaches that the gods and lords here are idols. There is only one God (1 Cor. 8:4).

III. God is not changing or evolving (Ps. 90:2; Mal. 3:6). More than one group holds the concept of an evolving God. If God were evolving, He would not be complete at this moment; therefore, He would be in a state of deficiency.

IV. God is not, and never was, a man (except, of course, when the second Person of the Godhead was born here on earth as our Lord Jesus Christ). See Numbers 23:19 and Hosea 11:9. As stated earlier, Mormon doctrine teaches that God was once a man. There is a serious warning in Romans

  1:21-24 about making God into the image of man.
V. God does not have a body.
 A. The fact that we were created in the image of God (Gen. 1:27) does not mean He looks like us.
  1. Created in righteousness and holiness (Eph. 4:24)
  2. Created in knowledge (Col. 3:10)
  3. God's likeness is righteousness (Ps. 17:15)
 B. God exists in His natural essence as a Spirit Being (John 4:24). Jesus stated that a being existing as a spirit does not have a body (Luke 24:39). This does not remove the fact that Jesus is indeed God in the flesh (1 Tim. 3:16; John 1:14), and the only way anyone has seen God is through the Person of Christ (John 1:18; 14:9). The only way God can be said to have a body is because God, the Son, now has a body.
 C. Mormons try to prove God has a body by quoting verses that speak of the hand, arm or eyes of God. That same logic, if followed to its logical conclusion, can be used to show that God is a bird (Ps. 91:4). Of course, God is not a bird, but the Bible does use figurative language to describe characteristics of God, such as hand, arm or eyes.
 D. God is invisible (1 Tim. 1:17).

Holy Spirit

 Explanation: Mormons make the claim that the Holy Spirit ("the Father's influence") and the Holy Ghost ("a person") are different, because the King James translation uses both phrases; yet, Spirit and Ghost are translations of the same Greek word, *Pneuma*.
 I. The Holy Spirit is a Person possessing intellect (1 Cor. 12:8), will (1 Cor. 12:11) and emotions (Eph.

4:30). These are characteristics of a person, not an influence.
- A. He is given designations proper to a personality (John 14:16, 17).
- B. Associations of His name show He is a Person (John 16:14; Acts 15:28).
- C. Performs acts proper to a personality (Eph. 4:30).
- D. Distinguished from His gifts (Luke 1:35; 4:14; Rom. 8:26; 1 Cor. 12:8).

II. The Holy Spirit is God (Acts 5:3, 4). Peter stated that when Ananias lied unto the Holy Spirit, he lied to God.

III. We receive the Holy Spirit when we receive Christ.
- A. Jesus said the Holy Spirit would be given to those who believe in Him (John 7:37-39).
- B. If a person does not have Christ's Spirit, he does not belong to Him; therefore, one must receive the Spirit when he is born into God's family (Rom. 8:9).
- C. Paul taught that one receives the Holy Spirit when he trusts in Christ (Eph. 1:13).

Jehovah

Explanation: Who Jehovah is is one of the biggest controversies raging between true Christianity and the cults. For example, the Mormons teach that Jesus is Jehovah, but God the Father is not. The Jehovah's Witnesses teach that God the Father is Jehovah, but Jesus Christ is not. The fact is, the Bible teaches both God the Father and Jesus, as well as the Holy Spirit, are Jehovah. To set the record straight, we need to realize that the name "Jehovah" is not actually the true name of God. The Hebrew did not have any vowels in its original form; therefore, the actual name of God was *YHWH* or, transliterated another way into English, JHVH. The Jewish scribes, out of respect for God, did not want to pronounce His name in oral readings, so they said *Adonai* (the Hebrew word for Lord or Master) instead. Eventually, vowel markings were added to the Hebrew; but when the scholars came to the name of God, *YHWH*, they put in the vowel markings for *Adonai* instead. The result was Yehowah or Jehovah. Probably the actual name for God is Yahweh, but we cannot be certain. It is as if God on purpose protected His name from those who would defile it.

As you examine the following verses, it is important to note the way the King James translators showed the Hebrew names for God. For example:

God—Elohim
Lord—Adonai
LORD or GOD—Jehovah

I. Father is Jehovah.
   A. Jehovah says to Jesus Christ, "Sit thou at my right hand" (Ps. 110:1).
   B. Jehovah places our sin on Jesus Christ (Isa. 53:6).
II. Jesus Christ is Jehovah.
   A. Jehovah states that His cost was thirty pieces of silver (Zech. 11:13).
   B. Jehovah was to be pierced (Zech. 12:4, 10).
   C. Jesus states He is the I AM (John 8:58).
   D. Jehovah is the I AM (Exod. 3:14, 15).
III. Holy Spirit is Jehovah.
   A. In Psalm 95 Jehovah makes a statement (Ps. 95:7-11).
   B. The writer of Hebrews says the Holy Spirit was speaking (Heb. 3:7-11). (The same procedure can be used with Jeremiah 31:33 and Hebrews 10:15, 16.)

Jesus Christ

Explanation: The Bible teaches us that we can know

if a group of individuals are true believers by comparing their Jesus with the Jesus of the Bible (1 John 4:1-3). Who, then, is the Biblical Christ?

I. Misunderstood verses
   A. Christ is the firstborn. Therefore, according to the cults, He had a beginning (Col. 1:15). This misunderstanding is a result of ignorance of Old Testament customs. Jesus holds the firstborn position, which gives Him the authority over the household of the Father. It does not mean He is a created being.
   B. In the King James Version, Revelation 3:14 states Jesus is the beginning of the creation of God. This does not mean Christ was the first object to be created by God. Instead, we are taught that all creation finds its origin in Christ (Col. 1:16).
   C. Passages such as John 10:29 which state, in essence, "My Father . . . is greater than all . . ." should not be taken to mean the Father is more powerful or "more God" than Jesus Christ. It does state the relationship between Deity within the Being of God. It can also be understood in relation to Christ's earthly ministry, where the Man Christ Jesus was in total submission to the will of the Father.
   D. Jesus is the "only begotten" (John 3:16), but not because He had a beginning. Jesus was the only One to come from the presence of God the Father (John 3:13) to be uniquely born ("only begotten") of the virgin, having been conceived by the Holy Spirit (Luke 1:35).

II. Jesus is God.
   A. Thomas calls Him God (John 20:28).
   B. God the Father calls Him God (Heb. 1:8).

- C. Bible teaches that Jesus is the Word and the Word is God.
    1. The Word is God (John 1:1). There is a special section on this verse in the chapter, "Practical Helps," (page 109).
    2. The Word was made flesh (John 1:14). Jesus is God in the flesh (1 Tim. 3:16).
    3. The Word is the "only begotten" (John 1:14). The "only begotten" is Jesus Christ (John 1:18).
    4. The Word is King of Kings and Lord of Lords (Rev. 19:13, 16). Jesus Christ is King of Kings and Lord of Lords (1 Tim. 6:14, 15).

III. Jesus is not the brother of Satan.
   A. Satan was created (Ezek. 28:13).
   B. Jesus wasn't created—He is God. (See point II in this section.)

IV. Jesus was physically resurrected.
   A. Resurrection of Christ is part of the gospel message (1 Cor. 15:1-4).
   B. Without Christ's resurrection, there is no hope for our salvation (1 Cor. 15:12-19).
   C. It was not just a spiritual resurrection (Luke 24:39).

Trinity

Explanation: The word "trinity" does not occur in the Bible. It is simply a theological term that describes a Biblical fact. The doctrine teaches that God is one Being existing as three Persons. Each Person is distinct, but all three exist as one God. People have tried to analyze this doctrine unnecessarily. God by His very nature of being God exists as three Persons. To question why God exists as three Persons is just as absurd as questioning why a man has two arms instead of four. Man by his natural existence has two arms. God by His natural existence is three Persons.

I. The Trinity can be proven by placing verses that demonstrate each Person of the Godhead is God beside verses that teach there is only one God. Conclusion: God exists as three Persons.
II. Two important Trinity passages
   A. Old Testament (Isa. 48:16)
      1. In this passage, Jehovah is speaking. Jehovah states that Jehovah and His Spirit have sent Him.
      2. To prove the speaker is Jehovah, compare Isaiah 48:12 in which the speaker says, "I am the first, I am also the last," with Isaiah 44:6 where Jehovah states He is the first and the last. Therefore, the speaker must be Jehovah. (See the explanation in the section "Jehovah," [page 59], about the King James translation of the word Jehovah.)
   B. New Testament (Matt. 28:19)
      The key to this verse is the fact that the verse says "name," not "names." Therefore, the name of the one true God is the Father, the Son and the Holy Spirit.
III. Other important references
   A. Deuteronomy 6:4: "Hear, O Israel: The LORD our God is one LORD." The Hebrew word for "one" in this passage means a united one. The word translated LORD is Jehovah.
   B. John 10:30: "I and my Father are one." This passage does not mean one in purpose, as the cults mean it, but rather one in essence. The Father and the Son in their very essence are God. (The cults try to make the passage in John 17:21-23 show that what Christ meant was a oneness of purpose. In reality Jesus was

referring to our oneness within the Body of Christ. He did not say we would be deity as He and the Father are in Oneness, but through His indwelling Spirit we would have Deity dwelling within us. We would be made one through the indwelling Holy Spirit.)

C. First John 5:7: "For there are three that bear record in heaven, the Father, the Word, and the Holy Ghost: and these three are one."

Impressive as this verse may seem, it will have no real effect on the cults. The problem is that this verse lacks historic manuscript backing. It is not found in the majority of the Greek manuscripts or in the oldest ones. Regardless of your personal position, you must realize the cults are aware, in most cases, of the problems with this verse so they will disregard it.

Six

The Way of Salvation

Baptism

Explanation: While mode and method of baptism are important, this section will deal only with the question of whether baptism is necessary to accomplish, in whole or in part, God's plan of salvation.

I. Misunderstood verses
   A. Mark 16:16: "He that believeth and is baptized shall be saved; but he that believeth not shall be damned." Some claim that this verse teaches one must be baptized to be saved. It is true that he who believes and is baptized shall be saved, but the key to understanding the verse comes in the second phrase. The one who is damned is the one who does not believe, not the one who is not baptized. An evangelist once gave this illustration for comparison: "The one who gets on the train and sits down will arrive in Los

65

Angeles, but the one who does not get on the train will not arrive." Getting on the train is what determines that the individual will arrive in Los Angeles, not whether he sits down. A person can remain standing and still ride a train, but he will not be the most comfortable. A person can be on his way to Heaven because of trust in Christ, and not be baptized; but he'll lack the joy of being obedient to God in this area.

B. John 3:5: "Jesus answered, Verily, verily, I say unto thee, Except a man be born of water and of the Spirit, he cannot enter into the kingdom of God." It is difficult to believe, but there are some who claim that the phrase "born of water" means baptism. In the Greek, the word for "and" is *Kai*, and many good Bible scholars believe the word should be translated "even" in this case. This would make the phrase to read, "born of water even the Spirit." Doctrinally, this is consistent in the Gospel of John and in the Bible as a whole. There is also the thought that water refers to the written Word of God.

1. The Gospel of John
    a. The Spirit is spoken of as living water (John 7:37-39).
    b. Christ's Word cleanses us (John 15:3).
2. The rest of the Bible
    a. We are washed at the moment of salvation by the Holy Spirit (Titus 3:5).
    b. We are cleansed by the written Word of God (Eph. 5:26).
    c. We are born again through the Word of God (1 Pet. 1:23).
3. There is also another view that the water refers to physical birth (the water breaking)

and the Spirit refers to spiritual birth. The argument is taken from the context, especially verse 6 of John 3. The reasoning behind the view is this: You must be born physically to get into your earthly family. You must also be born spiritually to get into God's Heavenly family. I don't personally believe this to be the proper interpretation; but whatever position you take, the important point is that the verse does not refer to baptism.

C. Acts 2:38: "Then Peter said unto them, Repent, and be baptized every one of you in the name of Jesus Christ for the remission of sins, and ye shall receive the gift of the Holy Ghost." To understand this verse properly, one needs to realize that the phrase ". . . be baptized . . . for the remission of sins . . ." is an interjection in the sentence. What Peter said was "Repent, and ye shall receive the gift of the Holy Ghost." He interjected the other phrase, but his main thrust was in the repentance part. (See the section on the Holy Spirit [page 50].) What does the phrase "be baptized for the remission of sins" mean?

1. Original Greek: The Greek word translated "for" is *eis* and in this case should be translated "because." We are baptized because we have remission or forgiveness. All baptism does is picture for the world what has already taken place inside the person. Unfortunately, in dealing with the cults, you will find they do not easily accept this.

2. English translation: There is a way of understanding the English translation that will also help clear up the false concepts. The proper understanding of the English word

"for" in this verse can be illustrated by the phrase "wanted for murder." The person in question is not wanted "in order to" murder someone, he is wanted "because" he murdered someone. We are not baptized to receive forgiveness of sins, but because we have received forgiveness already.
3. The context shows the people were baptized after they received the Word (Acts 2:41).
4. Cornelius and his people were baptized after receiving the Holy Spirit (Acts 10:44-48).

D. Acts 22:16: "And now why tarriest thou? arise, and be baptised, and wash away thy sins, calling on the name of the Lord." By studying this verse in relationship to the other Bible passages on this subject, we understand that the washing away of sins is a play on words, and is linked with calling on the name of the Lord, not with being baptized (see Rom. 10:13). The Amplified Bible translates the last of the verse ". . . by calling upon His name wash away your sins." The footnote explains this translation is correct because of the adverbial participle of means. The Today's English Version reads, "Get up and be baptized and have your sins washed away by calling on his name." Calling on Christ's name is the means through which the two imperatives of baptism and sins forgiven have a right to be. My sins are forgiven because I have called upon the name of the Lord. I am also baptized because I have called upon the name of the Lord. Baptism should be a natural step of one who has just been saved; forgiveness of sins is the automatic result of trusting Christ (Acts 10:43).

E. Romans 6:4: "Therefore we are buried with him

by baptism into death: that like as Christ was raised up from the dead by the glory of the Father, even so we also should walk in newness of life." There are a few other verses in which the word "baptize" appears in the English translation. Since they are all explained in much the same way, we will deal with just this verse. It is important to remember that the word "baptism" is not a translation. It is what is known as a "transliteration" (matching sound for sound the proper letter from one language alphabet to another). Baptize is the transliteration of the Greek word *baptizo*. The literal meaning is to immerse or place one thing in another. Just because "baptize" is used does not mean it refers to water baptism. The verse properly translated reads, "Therefore, we are buried with him by being placed into death. . . ." There is a spiritual immersion, but nothing about water is ever said.

F. First Peter 3:21: "The like figure whereunto even baptism doth also now save us (not the putting away of the filth of the flesh, but the answer of a good conscience toward God,) by the resurrection of Jesus Christ." The verse itself clarifies the meaning, for it says baptism does not remove the sins of the flesh. Baptism does give the already born-again believer the knowledge he has been completely obedient to God's wishes for the newly saved person. The illustration is Noah's ark. Just as Noah came forth from the ark to new life, baptism is a picture ("the like figure") of what happens the moment we receive Christ. We come forth from the grave of sin and death to new life. There are those who try to make the phrase "filth of the

69

flesh" mean "dirt of the body," but a study of the word "flesh" as used by Peter and the rest of the Bible will discredit that position for this verse (1 Pet. 4:2).

II. Proper Biblical teaching
   A. Baptism is not a part of the true gospel (1 Cor. 1:17; 15:1-4).
   B. The forgiveness of sins comes through trust in Christ alone (Acts 10:43).
   C. The thief on the cross was not baptized (Luke 23:42-43). The argument that during that dispensation God had not commanded baptism is not valid. John the Baptist had been baptizing.
   D. The proper order is to believe on Jesus Christ for salvation, then be baptized after one is saved (Acts 8:35-37; 16:30-34).

Baptism for the Dead

Explanation: Mormons have a doctrine in which they are baptized for people who have already died. They believe that when a non-Mormon dies, he goes to hell, which they call a spirit prison. Non-Mormons in spirit prison are taught the truth of Mormonism by Mormons who have died and come down from Paradise. When a non-Mormon is ready to accept the truth of Mormonism, he's allowed to go up into Paradise if someone here on earth has been baptized in a temple for him. Therefore, Mormons do much genealogical research. They check into their past, find their dead ancestors and get baptized for them, just in case they are waiting to go up into Paradise. This is the Mormon doctrine, but what does the Bible teach?

I. Misunderstood verses
   A. First Peter 3:18-20 and 4:6: These verses do not teach a second chance after death. The key to

understanding these verses is to supply the correct translation using the word "now," which the King James Version translators left out. The result is this: Verse 19, ". . . preached unto the spirits [who are now] in prison." Christ preached by His Spirit through Noah to those who are now in prison, but the message was delivered through Noah while they were still alive. Verse 6, ". . . the gospel was preached also to them [who are now] dead. . . ." The preaching was when they were alive.

B. First Corinthians 15:29: "Else what shall they do which are baptized for the dead, if the dead rise not at all? Why are they then baptized for the dead?" There are two possible explanations for what Paul said here. In either case, as we shall see in a moment, the rest of the Bible contradicts the Mormon interpretation of this verse.
1. A cult of that day was preaching baptism for the dead, and Paul alluded to them to illustrate his point about the resurrection. (Compare his use of "we" and then his use of "they.")
2. When we are baptized, we witness to the fact that the dead will rise again (which is why we are placed down in the water and then come out). We are baptized on behalf of the dead in that we show they will rise again.

II. Proper Biblical teaching
A. Temples are not for today (Acts 17:24).
B. We are not to do genealogical research from a theological position (1 Tim. 1:4; Titus 3:9).
C. Baptism is not what saves one (1 Cor. 1:17; Acts 10:43). If it does not save a person, why do it for the dead?

    D. There is an impassable gulf between Paradise and hades (Luke 16:26). Even if one in hell would admit he was wrong, there is no way he could go up to Paradise.
    E. Judgment follows immediately after death (Heb. 9:27). There is no second chance.

Children of God

Explanation: There are people today, not only in certain cults but in other parts of the "Christian world," who believe everyone on earth is a child of God. Is that Biblical?

I. Misunderstood verses
    A. Acts 17:29: "Forasmuch then as we are the offspring of God, we ought not to think that the Godhead is like unto gold, or silver, or stone, graven by art and man's device." Mankind is the offspring of God only in the sense of creation. God created the first man and we are descendants of that man (Luke 3:38).
    B. Numbers 16:22: "And they fell upon their faces, and said, O God, the God of the spirits of all flesh, shall one man sin, and wilt thou be wroth with all the congregation?" Again this applies to creation, not to a relationship. When the relationship aspect is being expressed, the phrase is "Father of spirits" and only applies to those who have become sons of God. God only disciplines His sons—no others (Heb. 12:5-11).
    C. Malachi 2:10: The phrase, "Have we not all one father?" is quoted to prove we are all children of God. The next phrase in the verse explains this statement as applying to the creation of mankind: ". . . hath not one God created us?"
II. The Bible teaches that not everyone is a child of God.

A. Jesus informs the Pharisees they are of their father, the devil (John 8:44).
   B. God's wrath will fall on those titled the "children of disobedience" (Col. 3:6).
   C. Elymas, the sorcerer, was called a "child of the devil" (Acts 13:10).
III. The Bible teaches that each of us can become a child of God only by being born into God's family through faith in Christ.
   A. We become children of God when we receive Christ (John 1:12, 13). Verse 13 teaches we are born again at that moment.
   B. "... Except a man be born again, he cannot see the kingdom of God" (John 3:3).
   C. "Whosoever believeth that Jesus is the Christ is born of God..." (1 John 5:1). There must be a personal trust in Christ to be born again.
   D. "For ye are all the children of God by faith in Christ Jesus" (Gal. 3:26). The "all" of this passage are the Galatian Christians.

Eternal Security

Explanation: The Biblical position that once a person has been saved by God he will always remain saved has been misunderstood, not only by the cults but also by many others. The Bible does not teach the concept that once a person is saved he is free to sin. It does teach that once a person is saved there is still the possibility he may sin (and there are times he will), but the Lord is removing the desire to sin as the believer grows in Christ. As stated earlier, it is not our trust that saves us but the Person of Christ. Unless Christ can fail, we cannot lose our salvation.

I. Misunderstood verses
   A. Matthew 24:13: "But he that shall endure unto the end, the same shall be saved." This is a future setting for the tribulation period during

which the Church will be absent (1 Thess. 1:10 with Rev. 6:17). Jesus is informing Israel that the ones who remain true to God through the tribulation period will escape God's judgment at the end of the Tribulation, and enter the thousand-year reign of Christ (Luke 17:34-37). This verse does not mean a person could lose his salvation. The Biblical principle of 1 John 2:19 is that if he is truly saved, he will not leave the truth; he will endure unto the end. If he leaves he was not truly saved.

B. Galatians 5:4: "Christ is become of no effect unto you, whosoever of you are justified by the law; ye are fallen from grace." To say this verse means we can lose our salvation is to take only the phrase "fallen from grace" and ignore the rest of the verse. It is actually teaching that if one tries to get to God through keeping God's laws, one is leaving the principle of salvation by grace. Romans 11:6 teaches that one cannot mix grace and works to gain salvation. Galatians 5:5 teaches God's righteousness comes by faith. This verse is the reply to the idea that loss of salvation is implied in verse 4.

C. Hebrews 6:4-6: "For it is impossible for those who were once enlightened, and have tasted of the heavenly gift, and were made partakers of the Holy Ghost, And have tasted the good word of God, and the powers of the world to come, If they shall fall away, to renew them again unto repentance; seeing they crucify to themselves the Son of God afresh, and put him to an open shame."

   1. An important point is often overlooked about this Scripture passage. If these verses teach one can lose his salvation, they would also

teach one cannot be saved again (see vv. 4-6).
2. In verse 9 the writer of Hebrews states he is persuaded that the people he is writing to are not of the type described in verses 4-6, but are manifesting the true fruits of salvation.
3. There are different views on what verses 4-6 are actually saying. One explanation (which I personally believe) is that when a person comes to the point of true repentance under the leading of the Holy Spirit but refuses to accept Christ, that individual can never be brought again to that repentant position. By rejecting Christ after knowing Who He is, they have again, in a figurative way, hung Him on the cross in open shame.

D. Hebrews 10:26-29: "For if we sin wilfully after that we have received the knowledge of the truth, there remaineth no more sacrifice for sins, But a certain fearful looking for of judgment and fiery indignation, which shall devour the adversaries. He that despised Moses' law died without mercy under two or three witnesses: Of how much sorer punishment, suppose ye, shall he be thought worthy, who hath trodden under foot the Son of God, and hath counted the blood of the covenant, wherewith he was sanctified, an unholy thing, and hath done despite unto the Spirit of grace?"
1. The same approach taken with Hebrews 6:4-6 can be taken here. To understand Biblical salvation clearly and reject it does not remove the fact that Christ's substitutionary death is still the only answer.
2. The phrase "he was sanctified" of verse 29 is referring to Christ, not to the one rejecting the truth.

3. Hebrews 10:39 informs the readers they are not of the group who draw back after understanding the truth, but are of those who go ahead and trust Christ.

E. Second Peter 1:3-12
1. Verse 3—Speaking to Christians: "given . . . us all things. . . ."
2. Verse 4—First of all having already a knowledge of Christ in salvation (see v. 3), we also receive the promises of a new nature and deliverance from the flesh when we receive Christ. We are made "partakers of the divine nature" in the new birth (John 1:12).
3. Verses 5-7—"Besides this" or "for this reason." Now the emphasis is not on how we receive the divine nature, but how we develop it.
4. Verse 8—If one has made the items listed in this passage of Scripture a part of his life, he will not be barren in his Christian life, but fruitful.
5. Verse 9—The person of verse 9 is forgiven, but he has forgotten that he was purged from his sin. Therefore, he lives in it.
6. Verse 10—Make your salvation a firm, stable, solid experience. This will keep you from falling into sin.
7. Verse 11—Speaks of entering Heaven abundantly. It does not mean those of verse 9 will not enter (see 1 Cor. 3:11-15).

F. Second Peter 2:1-22
1. Verse 1—"The Lord who bought them." Christ's death is sufficient even for the false prophets and teachers, but that does not mean they are saved.
2. Verse 15—"Which have forsaken the right

way. . . ." To forsake something one has to be aware of its existence, but not necessarily a part of it.

3. Verse 18—Teaches that those who follow the false teachers do not totally escape the world ("almost" in Greek). They may have come apart from the world, but they return to it.
4. Verse 20—They may have a full knowledge of the facts of salvation, even to the point of believing these facts are true; but as we pointed out in the previous chapter, there is a big difference between just believing Christ can save and trusting Him to do so.
5. Verse 21—It is a terrible thing to reject Christ after fully understanding what He did on the cross.
6. Verse 22—As Dr. Paul Tassell, National Representative of the GARBC, said, "You can dress up a pig, but it is still a pig."

G. First John 1:6, 7: "If we say that we have fellowship with him, and walk in darkness, we lie, and do not the truth: But if we walk in the light, as he is in the light, we have fellowship one with another, and the blood of Jesus Christ his Son cleanseth us from all sin." Whatever these verses mean, they cannot mean that one can lose his salvation. Why? Because walking in the light does not mean living without sin; for if we are in the light, the blood of Jesus cleanses us from all sin. The cleansing is continual to the one who is in the light. In John 1:9 we are taught that Christ is the Light of everyone who is born on earth, but only those who are born into God's family will not flee the light (John 3:19-21). To claim you are a child of God and flee the light is to be a liar (1 John 1:6). To walk in the light is the natural result and the true reality of being a child of God. Therefore, 1 John 1:9 is not a condition of God's acceptance but the promise of it. If a true believer sins, he does not have to run from God; he can run to God in the complete assurance of his unconditional acceptance. There is no fear of salvation loss.

II. Proper Biblical teaching

A. Eternal life by its very nature is everlasting (John 3:15). If one could lose his salvation, it would be called temporary life instead of eternal life.

B. Jesus stated that those who are His are held in His hand and in God's hand, and no one can pluck them out of Their hands (John 10:27–29). Jesus said "no man," which means everyone, including the person being held in His hand.

C. Paul stated that nothing, including future events (things to come), can separate us from Christ (Rom. 8:38, 39).

D. Paul and Jude stated that once God started the process of presenting a person faultless before God's throne, He would finish the job (Phil. 1:6; see also Jude 24).

E. Because Jesus as our High Priest can never die again, He will always be there to intercede for us when we sin (Heb. 7:24, 25). With Him as our Lawyer, we can never lose in God's court (1 John 2:1).

F. The very fact that we become children of God when we receive Christ proves we cannot lose our salvation (John 1:12, 13). My son may disobey me, but he can never undo his relationship with me. He will always be my son.

Once an individual is born into God's family, he will always be a child of God.

Salvation—Works vs. Grace

I. The Biblical plan of salvation
  A. God is a holy God and will not accept sin (Lev. 19:2).
  B. Every person on earth has sinned, resulting in a falling far short of God's holy standards (Rom. 3:23; Ps. 14:2, 3). There was no hope for anyone to spend eternity with God unless God did something to remove the sin barrier.
  C. What God did was to send His Son, Jesus Christ, to die in our place and to be punished for our sins (John 3:16; Rom. 5:8-10; 2 Cor. 5:21).
  D. We must receive Jesus as our Savior in order to be with God. This means we must trust the resurrected Christ and Him alone to bring us into the presence of God (John 1:12; 14:6; Acts 4:12; Rom. 10:13).

II. The Bible teaches salvation is by grace through the channel of our faith completely apart from works (Eph. 2:8, 9).
  A. Our righteousnesses (deeds done to be right with God) are as filthy rags in God's eyes (Isa. 64:6).
  B. It is not through good deeds we do that we are made right with God (Titus 3:5).
  C. Grace and works are not to be put together in salvation (Rom. 11:6).

III. The Biblical position on the law
  The word "law" is misused by the cults constantly. They take the word "works" as used in the New Testament and try to make it apply to the Old Testament ceremonial law. This will allow them to

say they do not believe in salvation by works. Then they turn right around and use James 2:26 (which we will discuss just a few lines down) and make works a part of salvation. In order to present the proper Biblical position, we ought to examine each use of the word "law" by the New Testament writers. An example is Romans 3, which deals with the law—not in ceremony—but in that which teaches the holy standard of God.

A. The purpose of God's righteous standard found in His moral law was to teach us we were sinners, not to bring us salvation (Rom. 3:19, 20).
B. Since the law could not save us, there had to be a way to be right with God apart from the perfect life required by the law (Rom. 3:21).
C. The way to be right with God is through faith in Jesus Christ (Rom. 3:22-26).
D. The law of faith is not a new set of laws needed for salvation, but the simple fact that salvation is through faith in Christ Jesus (Rom. 3:27, 28).
E. When we establish the law through our faith (Rom. 3:31), we demonstrate the purpose of the law—not to save us, but to show us that we are sinners and that salvation must come from outside the law.

IV. James 2 (the cults' favorite passage)
Explanation: Faith is a vertical act witnessed by God resulting in the salvation of the individual. Works are horizontal and seen by men. This is the point of what James is saying. The key phrase is in verse 24—"Ye see." Works are in relation to what man sees. Faith is what God sees. The big mistake comes when the cults make works a necessary part of what God sees for an individual to be saved. The Biblical concept, "works prove an individual is

saved," is true when the proving is before men, but not before God. God does not need proof, He sees the faith.

A. James did not believe one earns salvation or he would not have written James 2:10: "For whosoever shall keep the whole law, and yet offend in one point, he is guilty of all." If a person sins only once in his entire life, he cannot make it to God through works.

B. The phrase ". . . can faith save him?" in James 2:14 of the King James Version could be more correctly translated ". . . can that faith save him?" The whole first part of James 2 deals with being a Christian in more than word only. If one is a true believer in Christ he will help the man who is hungry or has need. He will not do it because he is trying to be saved but because he is saved.
   1. True faith results in works (James 2:18).
   2. When a person has been saved he will perform good works as the natural result of God working in his life (Eph. 2:10).
   3. Good works are a result of salvation by faith. If a person claims to be saved and does not do good works, the faith he possesses was never truly placed in Christ, and therefore that faith cannot save him.

C. Abraham used as an example
   1. The Biblical explanation of Abraham's justification before God is found in Romans 4:1-5. Abraham was saved because he exercised faith in God.
   2. The Biblical explanation of Abraham's justification before men (not just for his day, but for all time) is found in James 2:21-24.
      a. Verse 21 of James 2 is a fulfillment of

verse 23. Verse 23 occurred before verse 21 (Gen. 15:6 and Gen. 22).
   b. Therefore, Abraham had God's righteousness before the act of verse 21 (see v. 23). He had no need to be justified before God. His justification was before men.

In a very real sense God was using the whole incident to teach Abraham an important lesson: Trust Me no matter what! When God used the phrase in Genesis 22:12, "now I know," He was saying it for Abraham's benefit. Being God, He already knew the outcome of the lesson.

V. Philippians 2:12: ". . . work out your own salvation with fear and trembling."
   A. Our salvation is a wonderful reality accomplished by a holy God. We are to have reverential respect ("fear and trembling") as we live our lives for others to see. There is a difference between a child having respect for his parents and fearing a stranger who is trying to hurt him. Because of Jesus Christ, one never needs to be afraid of God's judgment, but should always reverence and praise the God Who redeemed him.
   B. In verse 13 of chapter 2 we are again reminded it is God Who is doing the work.

Seven

Other Areas

Eternal Marriages

I. Mormon position
Mormons believe that when a couple is married in a Morman temple, that couple is married for time and eternity. They will exist together as husband and wife in both the spiritual and physical aspects of such a relationship throughout the eternal ages.

II. Biblical position
 A. Jesus stated there is no marrying or giving in marriage in Heaven (Luke 20:27-36). The Mormon reply to this is we do not marry in Heaven—we marry on earth, and it lasts through eternity. To make this reply is to ignore the entire context of the passage. Jesus was asked a question concerning a woman who had seven husbands, all of whom died in their turns before she died. The question was, "Who will she be married to in Heaven?" That is

when Jesus made His reply that the marriage relationship will not exist in Heaven.
B. For any disappointed couples who love their relationship very much, here is a word of encouragement. Although you will not be married in Heaven, you will have a much closer relationship with your partner of this life (a perfect relationship); however, it will be the same relationship all believers enjoy together (John 17:23). The beauty of this promise is that it can begin here on earth.

Lost Tribes of Israel

Explanation: British Israelism is a concept that is believed by both cult and non-cult individuals. Armstrongism is the most famous group that holds this position. British Israelism teaches that after the fall of the Northern Kingdom of Israel, the ten tribes would be scattered in the deportation. Eventually, Ephraim would become Britain and Manasseh the United States. What is the proper Biblical teaching?

I. Ephraim and Manasseh are two tribes of people—separate from each other. Historically, Manasseh did not come from Ephraim (U.S. from Britain).

II. Biblically, there are no lost tribes.
  A. Ephraim and Manasseh were present in the land one hundred years after the Assyrian deportation (2 Chron. 34:9).
  B. All twelve tribes were represented as present at the dedication of Zerubbabel's temple two hundred years after the Assyrian deportation (Ezra 6:17).
  C. Anna was of the tribe of Asher (Luke 2:36).
  D. Although there were people of each tribe scattered during both deportations, they still

retained identity as the twelve tribes (James 1:1).
III. Israel outside the land of Palestine is under a Biblical curse (Deut. 28:63-68). Therefore, if the United States and Britain were its descendants, they would not be receiving God's blessings.
IV. There is to be a literal rejoining of both the northern and southern tribes into one nation in the land of Palestine (Ezek. 37:21, 22). We saw the beginning of this in 1948 with the rebirth of Israel as a nation.

One Hundred and Forty-four Thousand

Explanation: Jehovah's Witnesses teach there will only be 144,000 individuals from their group who will be with Jehovah. The passage they use is Revelation 14:1-15.

I. The Biblical nature of the 144,000
   A. They are future. The only references to them are found in Revelation 7 and 14. Anything described in chapters 6 to 22 of Revelation falls under the category of "the great day of his wrath" (Rev. 6:17) and present-day believers are promised deliverance from God's "wrath to come" (1 Thess. 1:10). Since we have not yet been delivered out of this world (Rev. 3:10 and 1 Thess. 4:15-17), we must conclude that Revelation 7 and 14 are still future.
   B. They are to be virgin males (Rev. 14:4).
   C. They are to be of the nation of Israel or the Jewish race (Rev. 7:4).

None of the above concepts matches the Jehovah's Witness idea.

II. The 144,000 are not the only ones who will be in Heaven with God.
   A. There will be more than just 144,000 Israelites in Heaven. People of every race will be there (Rev. 5:9).

B. There will be a multitude no man can number around the throne of God (Rev. 7:9-17).

Preexistence

Explanation: Mormonism teaches that we all existed in a spiritual preexistence, born to "Mrs. God" before we were born on this earth. This is not to be confused with reincarnation, which will be dealt with later. Mormonism also teaches that some of the spirit children of which we were all a part did good deeds in the preexistence and some did bad deeds. All of this is supposed to affect how we are born on earth. What does the Bible teach on this subject?

I. Misunderstood verses
   A. Job 38:4-7: "Where wast thou when I laid the foundations of the earth . . . and all the sons of God shouted for joy?" The Mormons claim that the sons of God referred to here are spirit children born in the preexistence who will later be born as humans on earth. They also state that God's question implied Job was present before the foundation of the world.
      1. The context teaches otherwise. The question God asked Job was a negative question, implying Job was not present in creation; therefore, Job's opinion had to take second place to God's. Job 38:21 finds God pointing out to Job that he was not yet born.
      2. The use of the word "sons" here does not have to carry the meaning of literal birth, and there is no reason to believe from the passage that it does. The Man Christ Jesus is the only One to be uniquely born of the Father in the Virgin Birth, and then only in the sense that the Holy Spirit prepared a body in the womb of Mary for God the Son to indwell (John 3:16; Luke 1:35; Heb. 10:5).

Therefore, the use of the word "sons" in Job indicates identification of created beings with the God Who created them. There is no doubt that an angelic race separate from man did exist at the creation, but there are two important points to note about them:
   a. Angels are not to be linked with mankind—they are separate (Ps. 8:4, 5).
   b. Angels are created beings (Ezek. 28:14, 15).
B. Jeremiah 1:5: "Before I formed thee in the belly I knew thee. . . ." Mormons use this verse to try to prove that Jeremiah existed before he was conceived in his mother's womb. This verse is a simple declaration of the foreknowledge of God (Isa. 46:9, 10).
C. John 9:2: "And his disciples asked him, saying, Master, who did sin, this man, or his parents, that he was born blind?" Mormons make the claim that the disciples were aware of a preexistence doctrine or they would not have implied a man could be born blind for his sin. According to the Mormons, the sin had to occur in a preexistence before he was born. Again the answer is the foreknowledge of God. The disciples did not believe in a preexistence, but they were aware of the many Old Testament passages that taught God's foreknowledge and so believed that God could know a person's life ahead of time.

II. Biblical opposition to preexistence
   A. Jesus is the only Man Who has come from a preexistence (John 3:13). He is the only One Who could ascend to Heaven on His own power.
   B. Paul taught that the physical life comes first, then the spiritual; not the reverse (1 Cor. 15:46).
   C. When Romans 9:11 states, ". . . the children

being not yet born, neither having done any good or evil . . . ," it makes clear despite Mormon doctrine that we could not have existed in a preexistence doing either good or bad deeds.

Reincarnation

Explanation: The concept of reincarnation is so alien to the Bible that the cults who believe it will rarely use the Bible to attempt to prove their position. This position is mainly held by non-Bible cults. Reincarnation in its basic form teaches that all life is evolving, seeking a state of less suffering and moving to the point of no suffering. Hence, the concept of achieving peace within oneself is of great importance. This has opened the door for the meditation movement. The use of Bible verses in dealing with reincarnation will probably not bring immediate results with people who do not accept the Bible as an authority. We do not apologize for the Bible, and it is very important that we know what the Bible teaches; hence the verses listed below. The most profitable approach may rest in sharing the peace that God gives in salvation, and the comfort true believers receive in their daily lives.

I. The peace of God
  A. Peace in salvation (Rom. 5:1, 2)
  B. Peace in the Christian life (John 14:27; 16:33; Phil. 4:7; Col. 3:15; 2 Thess. 3:16)
II. The Biblical opposition to reincarnation
  A. People can only die once physically (Heb. 9:27).
  B. In the story of the rich man and Lazarus we are instructed that there is no way back (Luke 16:19–31).

There are Biblical exceptions to the above points. Examples would be the people Christ raised from the dead who most probably died later, and the fact that we all will be resurrected someday. The important point to note is that none of the exceptions fit into any kind of concept found in reincarnation.

    C. The fact that Jacob and Esau had done neither good nor evil before their births would remove the possibility of their living on this earth previously (Rom. 9:11).

Soul Sleep: Eternity vs. Annihilation

Explanation: Jehovah's Witnesses, among other cults, make the claim that there is no hell. Instead, they teach only annihilation for the lost. Consistent with this concept is the idea that when people die, they do not go to Heaven or hell. Instead, the soul supposedly sleeps in the grave. Jehovah's Witnesses claim the Hebrew word "sheol" and the Greek word "hades" mean only "grave." We can agree with them in the sense that these two words are translations of each other between two languages and, therefore, carry basically the same meaning. An example would be Psalm 16:10 where the English word "hell" is a translation of the Hebrew word "sheol." When the New Testament quotes this passage, the Greek word used is "hades" (Acts 2:27). We cannot agree that the two words mean "grave." In Greek mythology, hades was the unseen world and all the dead went there. It was not a place where people ceased to exist. As the Greek-speaking world spread, and there arose a need for a Greek translation of the Old Testament (the Septuagint), the word "hades" was selected as the translation of the word "sheol." The translators could not have thought the word "sheol" meant only the grave since they used the Greek word "hades." The King James Version translators' solution to wide use of the word "sheol" was to translate it "grave" or "hell," based on the context of the passage. Perhaps the best single translation of the word is the phrase "the place of the dead."

I. Misunderstood verses
   A. Psalm 6:5: "For in death there is no remembrance of thee: in the *grave* who shall give thee thanks?"
      1. The Hebrew word is "sheol" (the place of the dead).
      2. This verse means there is no remembrance or giving thanks with the physical tongue where other men might hear and benefit. It does not mean we will not be able to worship God in thanksgiving and praise after death.
   B. Psalm 31:17: "Let me not be ashamed, O LORD; for I have called upon thee: let the wicked be ashamed, and let them be silent in the *grave*.
      1. Again the Hebrew word is "sheol" (the place of the dead).
      2. The wicked are silent physically.
      3. They are also unable to send communication from the place of the dead (Luke 16:27-31).
   C. Ecclesiastes 9:10: "Whatsoever thy hand findeth to do, do it with thy might; for there is no work, nor device, nor knowledge, nor wisdom, in the *grave,* whither thou goest."
      1. Hebrew word "sheol" (place of the dead)
      2. The fact that anyone uses the book of Ecclesiastes to build a doctrine demonstrates his lack of understanding as to why the book was recognized as Scripture. God put Ecclesiastes in the canon of Scripture to reveal the way the natural man thinks (key phrases "under the sun," "I perceive," "I said in my heart," found in Eccles. 1:9, 17; 2:1). The natural man sees death as an end to all things (Eccles. 6:6).
   D. Isaiah 38:18: "For the *grave* cannot praise thee, death can not celebrate thee: they that go down

into the pit cannot hope for thy truth."
   1. Hebrew word "sheol" (place of the dead)
   2. The same simple explanation given earlier for Psalm 6:5 is the answer to Jehovah's Witnesses' position on this passage: Death limits the physical body's ability to speak forth praise.
E. First Thessalonians 4:13: "But I would not have you to be ignorant, brethren, concerning them which are asleep, that ye sorrow not, even as others which have no hope."
   1. Again the reference must refer to the physical body because of the Biblical teaching of conscious life after death (see next major point in outline).
   2. If this were the only passage concerning death, one might come to the same conclusion as many of the cults, but the Bible is filled with passages concerning death, and they must be taken into account.

II. Proper Biblical teaching on life after death
   A. The place of the dead (sheol) is a place of consciousness.
      1. There is conversation among those who are in hell (Isa. 14:9, 10; Ezek. 32:21).
      2. Jonah compares his conscious time within the great fish as being in hell itself (Jonah 2:2).
   B. Jesus said we are to fear God, Who can both kill and then cast into hell (Luke 12:5). There are two distinct occurrences here: death and hell.
   C. The thief on the cross was told he would be with Jesus in Paradise on the same day as his death (Luke 23:42, 43). There are some who try to make the word "today" link with the phrase, ". . . I say unto thee . . . ," so that the complete

statement would be, "I say unto thee today, you shall be with me in paradise." To do this is to ignore the context and how good Greek scholars have translated this passage throughout the centuries. The importance of the context is seen in the fact that Jesus is responding to the thief's desire to one day be in Christ's kingdom. Christ's answer to the thief is he will not have to wait; *today* he will be in Paradise.

D. James 2:26 teaches that the body without the spirit is dead, and 2 Corinthians 5:8 teaches that to be absent from the body is to be present with the Lord. (Of course, this is in reference to the saved individual.)

E. The martyred people of Revelation 6:9-11 are seen conscious around the throne of God.

F. The story of the rich man and Lazarus describes in exact detail the events following death (Luke 16:19-31).
   1. There are claims that this passage is a parable and is symbolic.
      a. This is not a general story, but one that involves a certain rich man and a certain beggar named Lazarus.
      b. Even if it was a parable, a parable is based on commonly understood facts known to people of the area.
      c. The reality of a symbol is always much worse than the symbol representing it.
   2. If this story is not true, then Jesus lied and purposely misrepresented what life after death is really like.

G. In a very serious passage found in Mark 9:42-48, Jesus taught clearly that an individual cast into everlasting hell does not simply burn up in a place that exists forever. Instead, hell is a place where the fire is not quenched (see Rev. 14:9-11). Such passages as 2 Thessalonians 1:9, which speak of everlasting destruction, are used by certain cults to support their view of non-existence after death. The important point to notice is that **the destruction is everlasting.** A person cannot exist in everlasting destruction unless he is forever being destroyed. He cannot simply burn up and cease to exist. This is a very sobering thought, and this is the burden we need to have for the dear people of the cults.

Eight

Practical Helps

Temporary Alternative to Discussion

We would be foolish to believe that every Christian is ready to meet cult members in a one-on-one discussion. This does not remove the responsibility of every Christian to prepare himself. Yet, what do you do until you are prepared. You do not want to be unfriendly and ruin the chances of another Christian to witness later on; but sometimes people from the cults are so forward that one is put in a position of either discussing both parties' beliefs or of closing the door. What can you do?

Here is a temporary solution until you are ready for a full discussion. Tell your visitors you are very happy they dropped by. You love the Lord Jesus very much, but at the present moment you are unable to talk with them. May you have their phone number? If you ask for their phone number, they will not feel that they have to start a conversation at that moment. You will also then have a contact for the time you feel ready to talk with them.

Proper Use of Anti-Cult Material

As we have already stated in the chapter on attitude, one has to be careful of the literature he hands out. Tracts and material that deal directly with a cult, mentioning the name of the cult and its founder, especially in a negative way, often do more harm than good if given during the initial contact.

There is a proper use of this material. If a person of the cults has come to the point where he sees that what he has been taught disagrees with the Bible, and wants to do some research, then the material can be quite effective. Another way to use it is if someone is starting to lean toward joining a cult and also wants some research material. Again, the important point in each case is that the Bible disagrees with the cult.

Some Christian groups or organizations seem determined to produce an attack attitude against cults. Our attitude toward these kinds of groups should be as Jesus said in Mark 9:38-40. They are not our enemies. They are brothers and sisters in Christ who have a different attitude than we do concerning the winning of cult members. We do not have to use their approach, but we can pray for them that God will be able to use them.

This book is designed to help you, the reader, to witness to cults, but it can only be the beginning of your preparation. Knowing the Bible is the key to reaching the cults for Christ.

Suggested Visitation Passages

Basically, up to this point, we have dealt with what to do if the cults come to your home. What do you do when you are on visitation and you knock on the door of a cult member? Actually, most of what we have already shared can be applied to a visitation call. However, there are differences.

First, you must initiate the discussion. You will want to establish the authority of the Bible, but you will not be able, as a guest, to lay down the rules as easily as when the discussion is in your home.

Secondly, in most cases the members of a cult you meet in door-to-door visitation will not be nearly as difficult to deal with as those who come to your door. Be courteous, and do not push them any more than you would want to be pushed if you were in their position.

The next question is: What passages should you use to open the conversation and make the contact? There are quite a few good passages such as Acts 16:25-34 and John 3:1-18. (John 3 is a good passage, for Jesus is dealing with a religious man; but anyone using this passage needs to be prepared to answer the cult's argument that John 3:5 is dealing with baptism.)

Perhaps the best opening passage is 2 Timothy 3:15, 16. Verse 15 teaches that the Biblical (Scriptural) way of salvation is through faith in Jesus Christ. Verse 16 teaches that the Bible (Scripture) gives us all we need to know about God and how to be right with Him. This passage will help you establish the authority of the Bible and will also open up the conversation to the way of salvation.

A concluding passage of Scripture as the conversation closes is 1 John 5:9-13. We discussed the use of this passage under "Closing Comments" in chapter 3 (page 43).

The Bible as far as Translated Correctly

What do you do when a Mormon makes the statement that a certain verse of the Bible is not translated correctly? Here is a simple three-point approach to such a statement.

1. Ask the Mormon, "Are you certain this particular verse under discussion is translated incorrectly?" This is an important question, for it forces the Mormon to make an exact statement concerning the verse under discussion, instead of a general remark

that the Bible is the Word of God only as far as it is translated correctly.

2. If the Mormon claims the verse under discussion is not translated correctly, then ask him what parts of the Bible are translated correctly and what parts are not. Follow this question with another question: "Do you only accept the verses that you feel agree with you?"

3. There are many verses that teach the Bible cannot become a book of error (example to be used: 1 Pet. 1:23). Ask him, "Are all those verses translated incorrectly?"

Point of No Discussion

There is a point at which it is no longer constructive to continue a conversation with a person of the cults. This point can come early in a conversation but usually comes toward the end. The point of no discussion comes when the cult person absolutely rejects Biblical authority and chooses his religion's teachings over the Bible. Once God's Word, the Bible, is rejected, true Christians have nothing left to share, for all we know about God is found within the Bible's pages. (We are not talking about a conversation with a member of a cult who does not hold the Bible as Scripture. In that case, use one of the three points given in chapter 2 about non-Bible cults to initiate the conversation [page 30]. We are talking about the moment when the cult person understands what the Bible says and rejects it for his cult teachings.)

When in a conversation you find yourself at the point of no further discussion, share honestly with the individual why the conversation cannot continue: he has chosen his religion over the Bible. If he cannot agree with your statement and believes the Bible teaches his position, you have not yet arrived at the point of no discussion; continue talking with him. If he agrees with your statement, you are at the point of no discussion. Tell him you love him in Christ and let the conversation end.

Ephesians 2:8 and 9 and the Mormons

There is a special way Ephesians 2:8 and 9 can be used with Mormons. It is quite effective in most cases, but it must be remembered that each Mormon may have his own way of explaining his doctrine. Therefore, when one uses this approach, he must be prepared to adapt it to each individual with whom he deals.

Mormons have basically two different salvations within their system of doctrine. The first salvation is "resurrection." It is by God's grace because (according to Mormon doctrine) Christ paid for Adam's sin, providing resurrection, and it is also a free gift to all men. An important point to remember is that the first salvation (resurrection) is to every man. The second salvation is called "exaltation." Exaltation, according to Mormonism, results in godhood and the presence of God. It is received because of the worthiness of each individual demonstrated by his good works through obedience to the Mormon gospel. Christ's atonement is involved with this concept, but only becomes effective as the Mormon demonstrates his worthiness through his good works.

We have asked Mr. Green to assist us again in this demonstration. Remember, not every conversation will be this complicated, but it always helps to be ready.

MR. GREEN: Would you explain to me how the Mormons believe an individual receives salvation into the presence of God?

MORMON MISSIONARY: We believe salvation comes through faith and obedience to the gospel of Jesus Christ.

MR. GREEN: You used the word obedience. What does that involve?

MORMON MISSIONARY: The gospel in its basic form is faith in Christ, repentance, baptism for the forgiveness of sins, and laying on of hands for the gift of the Holy Ghost.

MR. GREEN: Are there other things you must do?

MORMON MISSIONARY: Yes, temple work and mission work would be a part.

MR. GREEN: Then you believe salvation comes through the performance of good works?

MORMON MISSIONARY: Good works are certainly a part, but I don't know if I would say good works save us. The Book of Mormon teaches that we are saved by faith after all we can do.

MR. GREEN: According to what you just said, you must work as hard as you can to qualify for the right to have faith to save you. Does that not make works necessary for salvation?

MORMON MISSIONARY: Well, yes, it would. James 2 says faith without works is dead.

MR. GREEN: The difference in the way you see that verse and the way I see it is that you believe faith is insufficient without works. I believe that works are a result of true faith.

MORMON MISSIONARY: Then it is a case of your opinion versus my opinion.

MR. GREEN: Perhaps you would be right if James 2 were the only passage dealing with the subject. Romans 11:6 informs us you cannot mix grace and works, and Ephesians 2:8 says, "For by grace are ye saved." What does the Bible mean when it says we are saved by grace?

MORMON MISSIONARY: We believe there is more than one type of salvation. Probably what is being spoken of here is resurrection.

MR. GREEN: Do you believe everyone will be resurrected?

MORMON MISSIONARY: Yes.

MR. GREEN: Then what do you do with the next phrase "through faith"? The verse says, "For by grace are ye saved through faith." Will only those who have faith be resurrected?

MORMON MISSIONARY: No, everyone will be resurrected.

MR. GREEN: What do you do with the verse?

MORMON MISSIONARY: I'm not sure. Perhaps I was mistaken. It may be this verse refers to exaltation. Faith is the first step in exaltation.

MR. GREEN: Are there other steps?

MORMON MISSIONARY: Well, yes.

MR. GREEN: What are they?

MORMON MISSIONARY: I've already mentioned them: repentance, baptism, receiving the Holy Ghost and so on.

MR. GREEN: Then exaltation is the salvation we spoke of already which is received through faith, and by doing the works the Mormon church says to do.

MORMON MISSIONARY: Yes, that is correct.

MR. GREEN: Ephesians 2:8 and 9 reads, "For by grace are ye saved through faith; and that not of yourselves: it is the gift of God: not of works, lest any man should boast." The last part of this verse contradicts your second salvation known as exaltation, because it states it is "not of works." No matter which salvation you choose, these verses in Ephesians 2 contradict your choice.

MORMON MISSIONARY: I said earlier that works do not save us. Faith saves us. We do the works to demonstrate our faith.

MR. GREEN: Is faith all you need for salvation?

MORMON MISSIONARY: No, you need to prove your faith by doing other things.

MR. GREEN: Then works are necessary?

MORMON MISSIONARY: Yes, but it still is faith that saves us.

MR. GREEN: How do you receive forgiveness of sins? By faith alone?

MORMON MISSIONARY: No, by baptism.

MR. GREEN: How do you receive the Holy Ghost? By faith alone?

MORMON MISSIONARY: No, through the laying on of hands.

MR. GREEN: You believe you can become a god. How do you become a god? By faith alone?

MORMON MISSIONARY: No, through obedience to the laws and ordinances of the gospel of Christ.

MR. GREEN: Are forgiveness of sins, receiving the Holy Ghost and exaltation, or becoming a god, part of salvation?

MORMON MISSIONARY: Yes.

MR. GREEN: I don't understand. You say that all of these things are part of salvation, and you say that faith saves you, but faith does not accomplish the things I just listed. What exactly does faith accomplish?

MORMON MISSIONARY: It is the most important thing. It gives meaning to everything else we do.

MR. GREEN: But faith alone cannot save?

MORMON MISSIONARY: That is correct.

MR. GREEN: Ephesians 2:8 and 9 says we are saved by grace through faith apart from works. I believe you must decide between the Mormon doctrine of salvation, which is faith plus works, and what the Bible says in Ephesians 2:8 and 9. The Bible leaves no in-between.

John 1:1 and the Jehovah's Witnesses

Without much difficulty, the "Word" mentioned in John 1:1 can be shown to mean Jesus Christ. John 1:14 teaches the Word was made flesh and is the only begotten of the Father. Hence, we know the Word is Jesus. Therefore, John 1:1 clearly teaches Jesus (the Word) is God. It reads, "In the beginning was the Word, and the Word was with God, and the Word was God." It is here the Jehovah's Witnesses step in and say this is not a correct translation of the Greek. In their New World Translation they translate the last phrase, "... and the Word was a god." They claim they are following a basic Greek rule which does exist. The rule is that when a noun lacks the definite article, it is not to be translated with the article "the"; instead, it is to be translated with the article "a." The word "Theos" (God, in this case) does lack the definite article, so their translation is "a god." Nevertheless their translation is incorrect.

Colwell's Greek rule states that when the predicate part of the sentence comes before the subject as it does in John 1:1, the predicate must be translated with a disregard to the lack of the definite article. Hence, the translation "... the Word was God," not "... the Word was a god."

Another problem for the Jehovah's Witnesses is that if they insist that this translation should be "a god," it would contradict their theology that there is only one God.

Nine

Why Witness to Religious People?

There are nearly five million Mormons in the world today. By their own statistics, every two and one-half minutes someone in the world becomes a Mormon. In addition to the Mormons, there are countless other cults growing rapidly through the world. We cannot ignore them and hope that someday they will go away. The next person becoming a Mormon may very well be your daughter or father or wife or even you. The people of the cults are good people who live moral lives. Yet, the Bible teaches this is not enough. They must come to the Biblical Christ in order to make it to God.

The world is filled with many religions, whether we call them cults, religions, Christian or pagan. The Bible warns that there are barriers a religion creates, preventing its people from being with God when they die. The barriers are obvious:

1. **False doctrine (1 Tim. 4:1)**

2. **False gospel (Gal. 1:6-9)**
3. **False Bible (2 Cor. 2:17)**
4. **False Jesus (2 Cor. 11:3, 4)**
5. **False apostles (2 Cor. 11:13-15)**
6. **False prophets (Matt. 24:11)**
7. **False godliness (2 Tim. 3:5, 7)**

In 1 John 4:1 we read, "Beloved, believe not every spirit, but try the spirits whether they are of God: because many false prophets are gone out into the world."

We have a very real responsibility not to accept at face value what anyone says is Biblical. We must examine every Jesus that is presented to us in the light of Who the Biblical Jesus really is. If the one sharing with us his personal belief has a false Jesus, we are not to hate and ridicule him. We are to present the real Christ in love, even though he rejects our message (Ezek. 2:3-5). Why? Because if it were not for the grace of God, we could be as he is.

Appendix

Letters to Mormons

What you are about to read are two letters I wrote to two different Mormons. In many ways they are a review of the principles this book teaches. They may help the reader see the principles in action. The first letter is in response to a letter I received from a Mormon missionary who attended one of my presentations on Mormonism. The second letter is in response to one from a Mormon teenage girl who had read my visitor signature in the guest book at Temple Square in Salt Lake City, Utah. After my name, I had written the following verses: John 3:16; Acts 16:31; Romans 3. She read the verses, took down my address and wrote me a letter explaining why I was wrong. Then she shared with me why she believed works must be a part of salvation. She referred to James 2:20 in order to try to prove her position.

In both of these letters, the names of the actual people involved have been changed.

Dear Mr. Young:
    I want to thank you for your honest approach. Some

of the things you shared have helped me to further understand what you believe. It really doesn't matter, though, in the final analysis what either of us believes. The most important thing in our lives isn't how sincerely we believe what we believe, but what the truth of God is.

Mr. Young, there is a real barrier between the two positions that we hold, and it must be faced before either position can be met. The barrier is the Bible itself. We both believe the Bible is God's Word: I, without condition, you, as far as it is translated correctly. This is our common ground for discussion. Our disagreement comes in its major form in your additional "scripture." The reason for the additional scripture is really twofold, according to your position. The reasons are continual revelation and the belief that the truth of God was lost about the second century and needed to be restored through Joseph Smith. I would like to examine both of these in the light of what the Bible says.

The most important thing in approaching the Bible is to forget everything you were taught about it and take it for what it actually says. That means when you read the verses I am about to share, forget your "LDS" position and my "Baptist" position, and ask yourself what it really says.

Was God's truth lost from this earth? In your letter, you shared verses about a "falling away" that would come. I agree with you in this, but let's be honest about what the verses say. There is no statement in any of the verses that when the "falling away" occurred, it would be so complete that there would not be one individual who truly knew God in God's way.

The Bible makes some interesting statements. In Psalm 100:5 we read that God's "truth endureth to all generations." The verse doesn't say a form of truth endures, but that it is the Lord's truth that endures. Now, let's think it through. If the truth of God endures to every generation, there will always be someone in each generation who has it. Since it cannot be lost, it does not need to be restored. Think through what the verse teaches. See also Isaiah 59:21; 40:8. Our very salvation and how we know we have it depends on the fact that the Bible did not become corrupt (1 Pet. 1:23-25).

The next question is the need for continual revelation. Does the Bible teach that? First, the Bible did come into existence through revelation and God did use prophets to do that, but in Hebrews 1:1, 2, we are taught that with the coming of Jesus Christ, the age of the prophets was coming to a close. God used the apostles and the last of the prophets to be the foundation of the Church, not to be the building (Eph. 2:19-22). What these men of God recorded for us is the "sure word" upon which we are to build. This "sure word" is the written Scripture of the Bible (2 Pet. 1:19-21).

In John 16:13 Jesus made an interesting statement. He said, "Howbeit when he, the Spirit of truth, is come, he will guide you into *all* truth. . . ." Jesus is speaking to His disciples. If we take the verse for what it actually says, it would mean that by the death of the last disciple present, we would have the *all* truth of God. Therefore, with the death of John, the apostle, we had God's complete Word. The Bible teaches the Holy Spirit is at work today also, but not in the work of giving revelation. He indwells a person when the person trusts Christ to bring him to God (John 7:37-39). He convicts the world of their sin of not trusting Christ, of the need to be right with God, of the fact of the coming judgment (John 16:7-11). The work of the Holy Spirit is very important, but the fact from the Bible that the Holy Spirit is not giving revelation today rests in the Bible's completeness, and the fact that our faith was once for all delivered unto us (Jude 3). Once again the Bible makes clear this was not a repeated thing.

In 2 Timothy 3:15, 16 the Bible again points to the fact that it is Scripture that teaches us how first we can know we are saved, and then how to serve God. It is the Bible that teaches us all we need to know about God (that's doctrine), where we are wrong (reproof), how to correct the wrong (correction), how to be right with God (instruction in righteousness). Therefore, it must be used to teach us how to be with God. I know I've spent a long time on this one point, but it is the very basis for the difference between us. If, then, the Bible is the only authority that God has for today, what does it teach about salvation (i.e., the way to God)? First, it is not by any works done to be right with God (Titus 3:5; Isa. 64:6). It is not through baptism, for baptism is not a part of the gospel (1 Cor. 1:17). Baptism is for after we are saved to show to the world we are trusting Christ (Acts 8:35-37). Baptism does not bring forgiveness of sin because all the prophets of God state that forgiveness of sin comes through trusting Christ (Acts 10:43). Any verses that have been used to "prove" otherwise have to be examined in the light of the rest of the Bible. Salvation is not the Mormon concept of exaltation (Isa. 43:10). (I say this with respect for your right to believe as you do.)

The Biblical concept of salvation is first that we can know we have eternal life (1 John 5:13), and this eternal life is the very presence of the Father in eternity given to us because we come to God through Jesus Christ (John 14:6; 1:12; 3:15-18).

In Ephesians 2:8 and 9 God's true salvation plan is given. Here we are taught we are saved by grace. This is not a concept of resurrection, for if that were true only those who have faith would be resurrected. The verse says "for by grace are ye saved *through faith."* Neither can the verse be teaching the Mormon concept of working one's way to God through obedience to the Mormon gospel, for the rest of the verse teaches that it is "not of yourselves: it is the *gift of God: Not of works,* lest any man should boast." The Bible teaches you cannot mix grace and works together in salvation (Rom. 11:6).

As I close my letter, I quote you. "I hope you are not offended by anything I have written." I wasn't. It is my desire that you will feel the same way. I learned from your letter. I studied it very carefully. The truth of God is the most important thing in our lives. Seek to know God's truth whatever the cost. May God direct in your study. I await your reply.

In Christian Love,
John T. Rogers

P.S. There were a few questions asked in your letter I would like to answer directly.

1. The restitution of *all things* in Acts 3:21 is exactly that and must apply to Christ's coming again, for Christ was to remain in Heaven until it occurred. Secondly, when it occurs, then everything will be restored to what it was. This is not talking about doctrine (i.e., the gospel and God's truth) for that cannot be lost (Ps. 100:5). What it is talking about is earth being restored to the direct rulership of God as it was before Adam and Eve sinned. This also in-

volves Israel being in their land and worshiping the true God (Ezek. 37:1-14). They are in the land today but are not worshiping the true God. Therefore the gospel (which has never been lost) can be preached in all nations before His coming to set up the millennial Kingdom.*

2. We do not believe the Bible teaches Jesus is the Father. We believe there is one God (Deut. 6:4) and that He is God alone. There is no other God on earth or Heaven above (Deut. 4:39). The Bible teaches that there is one God, but that He exists as three Persons. See Isaiah 48:16; Matthew 28:19. (Notice the word is name, not names. The name of God is the Father, the Son, and the Holy Ghost.)

Author's Note: Of course the Rapture will occur seven years earlier, and the gospel spoken of is the good news of the coming King.

Dear Karen:

I have just read your letter, and I wish to thank you for writing. Your letter was greatly appreciated. As I read your letter, I noticed that you stated several times that it is important to examine the context in order to understand what each verse means. I also noticed that you said we must take the entire train of thought of the New Testament before we can come to a conclusion. I agree completely with you in this. With this in mind we will do a reexamination of the verses in discussion. Before we do this, though, we must establish a basis for discussion. In simple words, what is going to be the evidence we use when we make a statement. Second Timothy 3:15-17 reads:

> And that from a child thou hast known the holy scriptures, which are *able to make thee wise unto salvation through faith which is in Christ Jesus.* All scripture is given by inspiration of God, and is profitable for doctrine, for reproof, for correction, for instruction in righteousness: That the man of God may be perfect, throughly furnished unto all good works.

From these verses we realize that it must be the written

Word of God and it alone that we use as an authority. In John 16:13 Jesus makes an interesting statement to His disciples:

> Howbeit when he, the Spirit of truth, is come, *he will guide you into all truth:* for he shall not speak of himself; but whatsoever he shall hear, that shall he speak: and he will shew you things to come.

The Holy Spirit, before the death of the apostles, would guide them into all truth. They then had the responsibility to relate the all truth they received from the Holy Spirit to the people. This they did in their writings. We therefore have in the Bible the all truth which is profitable for doctrine, for reproof, for correction, for instruction in righteousness. There is no need for additional truth. Our faith was only given once.

> Beloved, when I gave all diligence to write unto you of the common salvation, it was needful for me to write unto you, and exhort you that ye should earnestly contend for *the faith which was once delivered unto the saints* (Jude 3).

In Psalm 119:140 we read:

> *Thy word is very pure:* therefore thy servant loveth it.

From this verse we learn that the Word of God is pure and uncorrupted. It guides in our daily lives.

> Thy word is a lamp unto my feet, and a light unto my path (Ps. 119:105).

Its power remains always and is with us today:

> Thy word is true from the beginning: and *every one of thy righteous judgments endureth for ever* (Ps. 119:160).

Jesus stated this in John 17:17:

> Sanctify them through thy truth: *thy word is truth.*

In Psalm 100:5 we read:

> For the Lord is good; his mercy is everlasting; and *his truth endureth to all generations.*

God's truth, which is the Word of God, endureth to every single generation. Therefore it could never be lost and there is no need for restoration of the truth. We are faced with only one conclusion—the Bible must be our sole authority. How do we avoid a misunderstanding of it? Listen to these verses:

> For the preaching of the cross is to them that perish foolishness; but *unto us which are saved it is the power of God* (1 Cor. 1:18).
>
> God, who at sundry times and in divers manners *spake in time past unto the fathers by the prophets, Hath in these last days spoken unto us by his Son*, whom he hath appointed heir of all things, by whom also he made the worlds (Heb. 1:1, 2).
>
> *No man hath seen God at any time;* the only begotten Son, which is in the bosom of the Father, *he hath declared him* (John 1:18).

Unless someone is saved through a personal relationship with Jesus Christ by faith, he cannot understand the things of God. God once used prophets, but now He uses His Son Who fulfilled the words of the prophets; and if we trust Him to save us, through Him we can understand the Word of God. Now we will go to the verses in discussion.

In John 3 Nicodemus wants to find out more about Jesus:

> There was a man of the Pharisees, named Nicodemus, a ruler of the Jews: The same came to Jesus by night, and said unto him, Rabbi, we know that thou art a teacher come from God: for no man can do these miracles that thou doest, except God be with him (John 3:1, 2).

Before any further discussion, Jesus gets right to the point:

> Jesus answered and said unto him, Verily, verily, I say unto thee, *Except a man be born again, he cannot see the kingdom of God* (John 3:3).

Jesus states there is only one condition for entering the kingdom of God, and that is to be born again. This really confuses Nicodemus as we see in the next verse.

> Nicodemus saith unto him, How can a man be born when he is old? can he enter the second time into his mother's womb, and be born? (John 3:4).

This is a logical question, and Jesus answers it:

> Jesus answered, Verily, verily, I say unto thee, Except a

man be *born of water and of the Spirit*, he cannot enter into the kingdom of God (John 3:5)

If you will recall, this is the verse you wanted me to examine. What does it mean to be born of water and (of) the Spirit? (The word "of" was put in by the King James Version translators. That is why it is in italics in your Bible.) To be born of water and the Spirit cannot mean to be baptized, for if that was what Jesus meant He would have said "baptized." Then what does this verse mean? The answer is found in the following verses:

> In the last day, that great day of the feast, Jesus stood and cried, saying, *If any man thirst, let him come unto me, and drink.* He that *believeth* on me, as the scripture hath said, *out of his belly shall flow rivers of living water.* (*But this spake he of the Spirit*, which they that *believe* on him should receive: for the Holy Ghost was not yet given; because that Jesus was not yet glorified.) (John 7:37-39).

> Not by works of righteousness which we have done, but according to his mercy he saved us, *by the washing of regeneration, and renewing of the Holy Ghost* (Titus 3:5).

From these verses we learn that the word "water" means a spiritual cleansing through the Holy Spirit. In John 3:5 the Greek word for "and" can be translated "even." The result is "born of water even the Spirit." What does the Holy Spirit use to bring about this spiritual cleansing? The Bible tells us this tool is the Word of God:

> Now *ye are clean through the word* which I have spoken unto you (John 15:3).

> Being born again, not of corruptible seed, but of incorruptible, *by the word of God*, which liveth and abideth for ever (1 Pet. 1:23).

> That he might sanctify and cleanse it with *the washing of water by the word* (Eph. 5:26).

As we continue in John 3, we read this in the next two verses:

> That which is born of the flesh *is flesh;* and that which is born of the Spirit *is spirit*. Marvel not that I said unto thee, Ye must be born again (John 3:6, 7).

One might ask after reading this verse, "Which comes first—the spiritual birth or the natural birth?" The answer is found in 1 Corinthians 15:46:

> Howbeit that *was not first* which is spiritual, but that which is natural; and *afterward* that which is spiritual.

In John 3:8 we learn that the spiritual birth is done through the Spirit in a wonderful and mysterious manner:

> The wind bloweth where is listeth, and thou hearest the sound thereof, but canst not tell whence it cometh, and whither it goeth: *so is everyone that is born of the Spirit.* Nicodemus answered and said unto him, How can these things be? Jesus answered and said unto him, Art thou a master of Israel, and knowest not these things? Verily, verily, I say unto thee, We speak that we do know, and testify that we have seen; and ye receive not our witness. *If I have told you earthly things,* and ye *believe* not, how shall ye *believe, if I tell you of heavenly things?* (John 3:8-12).

Up until now Jesus has been using earthly illustrations to demonstrate Heavenly things. Just as you are born into your family, you must also become a child of God through a spiritual birth. You must be "born again." The Bible does not teach that everyone is a child of God. In Ephesians 2:1-3 we find we all were by nature the children of wrath and the children of disobedience. In Romans 9:8 we read:

> That is, They which are *the children of the flesh,* these are *not the children of God.* . . .

In John 8:39-47 Jesus calls the Pharisees children of Satan when He states, "Ye are of your father, the devil." The Bible teaches that we are all children of Satan, and we need to be born into God's family. How this is done is found in John 1:12 and Galatians 3:26.

> But as many as received him [Jesus], to them gave he *power to become* the sons of God, even to them that *believe* on his name: Which were born, *not of blood, nor of the will of the flesh,* nor of the will of man, but of God (John 1:12, 13).

> For ye are all the children of God *by faith in Christ Jesus* (Gal. 3:26).

In John 3:13 we learn that Jesus is the only One Who came from Heaven to take upon Himself the flesh of man:

> And no man hath ascended up to heaven, *but he that came*

> *down from heaven, even the Son of man* which is in heaven.

In John 1:1 we find that the Word is God:

> *In the beginning was the Word,* and the Word *was with* God, and the Word *was* God.

In John 1:14 God being the Word was made flesh:

> And the *Word was made flesh,* and dwelt among us, (and we beheld his glory, the glory as of *the only begotten of the Father,*) full of grace and truth.

God was made flesh so that He could die on the cross for our sins (Rom. 5:8; 1 Cor. 15:1-4). The Bible teaches us that there is only one God in the universe and throughout all eternity (Deut. 6:4; Ps. 90:2; Isa. 43:10, 11; 44:6, 8; 45:5, 22). It also teaches that God is not a man and that He is not in human form (Num. 23:19; Job 9:32; Hosea 11:9; John 4:24; Luke 24:39; John 1:18; 5:37; Matt. 16:17). The Bible also states that the Father, the Son and the Holy Spirit are each God and that they are the same God for, remember, there is only one God (1 Thess. 1:1; Isa. 9:6; John 1:1; Heb. 1:8; Isa. 44:6; Rev. 1:5-11; John 1:23; Isa. 40:3; Mark 1:24; Isa. 54:5; Hosea 11:9; Gen. 1:26;* Isa. 48:16; Matt. 28:19;** John 5:18; 14:7-11; 10:30; 17:5). God is not evolving to a higher state (Mal. 3:6; Heb. 13:8).

I realize that I have just thrown quite a list of verses at you and that there might be a strong temptation to bypass them, but I strongly suggest that you look each of them up so that you will understand that my statements are Scriptural. Now we will return to John 3. Jesus explains His coming death on the cross:

> And as Moses lifted up the serpent in the wilderness, even so must the Son of man be lifted up (John 3:14).

Why?

> That whosoever *believeth* in him should not perish, but have *eternal life* (John 3:15).

---

*The image of God here is righteousness, not physical appearance (Eph. 4:24; Col. 3:10).
**Notice it states "name," not "names."

The good news of the gospel:

> For God so loved the world, that he gave his only begotten Son, that whosoever *believeth* in him should not perish, but have everlasting life. For God sent not his Son into the world to condemn the world; but that the world through him might be saved (John 3:16, 17).

The condition for being lost or saved is believing in Jesus Christ as your personal Savior:

> He that *believeth* on him is not condemned: but he that *believeth not* is condemned *already*, because *he hath not believed* in the name of the only begotten Son of God (John 3:18).

In verse 36 at the end of the chapter we have a brief summary:

> He that *believeth* on the Son *hath* everlasting life: and he that *believeth not* the Son *shall not see life;* but *the wrath of God abideth on him* (John 3:36).

Now, let's turn to that passage in Acts 16:31. The jailer has just asked Paul and Silas a very important question: "What must I do to be saved?" Paul answers, "Believe on the Lord Jesus Christ, and thou shalt be saved, and thy house." This is the only condition placed on salvation. According to Paul, if a person believed, he would be saved. You mentioned that in verse 33 the jailer was baptized. This is true, but the baptism did not save him and was not necessary for salvation. The jailer was baptized because he had trusted the Lord Jesus to save him and wanted to show this fact to the world. In Acts 10:43 we read:

> To him [Jesus] give all the prophets witness, that through his name whosoever *believeth* in him *shall receive remission of sins.*

A belief and trust in Jesus brings about the forgiveness of sins without baptism. It is through His blood our sins are forgiven:

> And almost all things are by the law purged with blood; and *without shedding of blood is no remission* (Heb. 9:22).

> But if we walk in the light, as he is in the light, we have fellowship one with another, and *the blood of Jesus Christ his Son cleanseth us from all sin* (1 John 1:7).

> Surely *he hath born our griefs*, and *carried our sorrows:* yet we did esteem him stricken, smitten of God, and afflicted. But *he was wounded for our transgressions, he was bruised for our iniquities:* the chastisement of our peace was upon him; and *with his stripes we are healed.* All we like sheep have gone astray; we have turned every one to his own way; and *the LORD hath laid on him the iniquity of us all* (Isa. 53:4-6).

> Much more then, being now justified *by his blood,* we shall be *saved from wrath* through him (Rom. 5:9).

> In whom *we have redemption through his blood,* even *the forgiveness of sins* (Col. 1:14).

Many people have the mistaken idea that Acts 2:38 means that baptism brings about the forgiveness of sins. The Greek word translated "for" should have been in this case translated "because of." The verse should read: "Then Peter said unto them, Repent, and be baptized every one of you in the name of Jesus Christ because of remission of sins. . . ." People were baptized because they had trusted Jesus to forgive them their sins. This is explained in context in verse 41:

> Then they that gladly *received his word* were baptized: and the same day there were added unto them about three thousand souls (Act 2:41).

The Bible tells us that Jesus is our High Priest and holds an intransmissable Priesthood (Heb. 7:22-25). Because priests died in the Old Testament, there was a necessity for a changeable priesthood. But Jesus lives forever to make intercession for us if we come to Him. Therefore, He is able to save us because of His death and resurrection (Heb. 10:11, 12). For an example of Jesus forgiving sins, read Luke 7:36-50.

There is also another reason to believe that baptism has nothing to do with salvation or the forgiveness of sins. In 1 Corinthians 1:17 Paul states:

> *For Christ sent me not to baptize, but to preach the gospel:* not with wisdom of words, lest the cross of Christ should be made of none effect.

The gospel has nothing to do with baptism. First Corinthians 15:1-4 tells us what the gospel is. In verse 14 of 1

Corinthians 1, Paul makes this pronouncement:

> I thank God that I baptized none of you, but Crispus and Gaius (1 Cor. 1:14).

If baptism were necessary for salvation, why did Paul make such a statement? He came not to baptize, but to preach the good news of Christ's death, burial and resurrection; how we might be saved through faith in the shed blood of the Lord Jesus Christ.

Now, I think it is time we take a look at Romans 3. Before we do this, though, I want you to think about something seriously for a moment. You have never met me or discussed theology with me. Yet, by reading this chapter, you came to the conclusion that I believe in salvation by grace. Now, it could not have been me who gave you this conclusion for we have never met. Therefore, it had to be the chapter you read that brought you to the conclusion that I believe in salvation by grace. The Bible does teach salvation by grace. Listen to these verses:

> *For by grace are ye saved through faith;* and that *not of yourselves:* it is *the gift of God: not of works,* lest any man should boast (Eph. 2:8, 9).

The Bible teaches us that no one on earth does any good in himself. In fact, it teaches that everyone is a sinner and that all are bad. Read again Romans 3:10-18. The Bible teaches that there is no good in man:

> For I know that in me (that is, in my flesh,) *dwelleth no good thing:* for to will is present with me; but *how to perform that which is good I find not* (Rom. 7:18).

We also learn that there is none righteous in God's eyes:

> God looked down from heaven upon the children of men, to see if there were any that did understand, that did seek God. *Every one of them* is gone back: *they are altogether* become filthy; *there is none* that doeth good, no, *not one* (Ps. 53:2, 3).

In Isaiah 64:6 we learn that our righteousnesses, our good deeds done to be right with God, are filthy rags in God's eyes. Therefore our goodness, our righteousness cannot get us into the presence of the Father. Then why was the law given if we cannot enter God's presence through it? Romans 3:19, 20 has the answer:

> Now we know that what things soever the law saith, it saith to them who are under the law: that every mouth may be stopped, and *all the world may become guilty before God*. Therefore by the deeds of the law there shall *no flesh be justified* in his sight: for by the law is the knowledge of sin.

The law was given to make us realize that we were sinners and that we could not save ourselves (John 3:19, 20; Gal. 3:24). Since we cannot save ourselves and since our righteousness is as filthy rags, we have to have God's righteousness to gain the presence of God.

> But now the *righteousness of God* without the law is manifested, being witnessed by the law and the prophets; even *the righteousness of God which is by faith of Jesus Christ unto all and upon all them that believe:* for there is no difference: *for all have sinned, and come short of the glory of God* (Rom. 3:21-23).

> But *your iniquities have separated between you and your God*, and your sins have hid his face from you, that he will not hear (Isa. 59:2).

> And be found in him, *not having mine own righteousness*, which is of the law, but that which is *through the faith* of Christ, *the righteousness which is of God by faith* (Phil. 3:9).

When a person puts his trust in Christ, the following happens:

> Being *justified freely by his grace through the redemption that is in Christ Jesus:* whom God hath set forth to be a propitiation *through faith in his blood*, to declare *his righteousness for the remission of sins* that are past, through the forbearance of God (Rom. 3:24, 25).

God withheld punishment for the sins of the people of the Old Testament who trusted in the coming Savior, knowing that when Jesus died, His shed blood would bring about the forgiveness of their sins. He did this in order

> To declare, I say, at this time his righteousness: that he might be just, and *the justifier of him which believeth in Jesus*. Where is boasting then? It is excluded. By what law? of works? *Nay:* but *by the law of faith* (Rom. 3:26, 27).

In Galatians we read that if we could have been saved by good works, there would have been no need for Christ to die (Gal. 2:16-21; 3:21, 22). We now must come to the same conclusion that Paul came to in Romans 3:28:

> Therefore we conclude that a man is justified by faith without the deeds of the law.

Before we examine James 2, there is something important that we must understand about God's grace (Greek: unmerited favor) toward man. It cannot work hand in hand with man's goodness to save him (Gal. 5:4, 5; Rom. 4:14). Be sure to check these references out. Now listen to this verse found in Romans 11:6:

> And if by grace, then is it no more of works: otherwise grace is no more grace. But if it be of works, then is it no more grace: otherwise work is no more work (Rom. 11:6).

If a person says he is going to earn his way into God's presence, he can expect no help at all from God. God will show no mercy in this case. Is it possible then for a man to be saved by his good works? NO! And here are three Bible reasons why:

1. According to James 2:10, if you sin in just one area, you are guilty of sinning in everything. "For whosoever shall keep the whole law, and yet *offend in one point,* he is *guilty of all.*" Jesus set up the same impossible standards when he said, "Be ye therefore perfect, even as your Father which is in heaven is perfect" (Matt. 5:48). The first thing one must do in order to earn his way into God's presence is to live a perfect life. This is impossible and no one has done it. "For all have sinned, and come short of the glory of God" (Rom. 3:23).

2. The second reason is found in Isaiah 64:6: "But we are all as an unclean thing, and *all our righteousnesses are as filthy rags;* and we all do fade as a leaf; and our iniquities, like the wind, have taken us away." Even if we could keep from sinning during our lifetime (which we can't), our good works would condemn us. The reason rests in the fact that our good works come from us and not from God.

3. The third thing to remember is the fact that we are born sinners. Even from the moment of conception we are in sin. "Behold, I was shapen in iniquity; and in sin did my mother conceive me" (Ps. 51:5).

"The wicked are estranged from the womb: they go astray as soon as they be born, speaking lies" (Ps. 58:3).

What about James 2? It is obvious from James 2:10 that James does not believe a person can be saved by keeping the law. In James 2:14 we read the following:

> What doth it profit, my brethren, though a man say he hath faith, and have not works? can faith save him? (The Greek reads: "can *that* faith save him?")

If anyone receives Jesus by faith as their personal Savior, the result is a new being created inside that person.

> Therefore, if any man be in Christ, he is a new creature: old things are passed away; behold, all things are become new (2 Cor. 5:17).

God works through this new creation we have become causing us to perform good works.

> For we are his workmanship, *created in Christ Jesus unto good works*, which God hath before *ordained* that we should walk in them (Eph. 2:10).

We cannot perform good works in God's eyes unless we are saved already and have Jesus living in us. Once God has begun this work inside us, He will continue it always until the day we are with the Lord and can no longer sin against Him.

> Being confident of this very thing, that he which hath begun a good work in you *will perform it until* the day of Jesus Christ (Phil. 1:6).

If a person trusts the Lord Jesus to save him, then Christ's blood which He shed on the cross gives the Holy Spirit the right to perform good works through the person.

> How much more shall the blood of Christ, who through the eternal Spirit offered himself without spot to God, *purge your conscience from dead works to serve the living God?* (Heb. 9:14).

A person who has been saved by a personal trust and faith in Jesus does good works, then, that are of God and not of man (John 3:21). Now we can begin to understand the point of what is being said in James 2:14. The faith that saves a person is a personal trust in Jesus Christ for salvation, resulting in good works being done through the Holy Spirit. We find this illustrated in Matthew 7:16-20. An unsaved person will not produce good fruit and will be cast into hell. A saved person will produce good fruit naturally as a result of being saved. There are a lot of people who claim they have faith in Christ, but their very actions deny the fact.

> They profess that they know God; but in works they deny him, being abominable, and disobedient, and unto every good work reprobate (Titus 1:16).

In James 2:17, 18 we read:

> Even so faith, if it hath not works, is dead, being alone. Yea, a man may say, Thou hast faith, and I have works: shew me thy faith without thy works, and *I will shew thee my faith by my works.*

The good works done through the Holy Spirit are an outward witness to man of the inward faith. There is a difference between believing the Bible is true and trusting in what it says. It is one thing to believe that Jesus died for all; it is more important and absolutely necessary for salvation that you believe He died for you personally.

> Thou believest that there is one God; thou doest well: the devils also believe, and tremble. But wilt thou know, O vain man, that faith without works is dead? (James 2:19, 20).

A faith that does not produce good works is dead in the eyes of men and worthless to man, for he sees no value in it. If a person has truly trusted Jesus to save him, he should want to do good works to demonstrate his faith to other men so that they might be saved also.

> This is a faithful saying, and these things I will that thou affirm constantly, that they which have believed in God might be careful to maintain good works. These things are good and profitable unto men (Titus 3:8).

In verses 21 and 22 we read how Abraham's works justified him before men:

> Was not Abraham our father justified by works, when he had offered Isaac his son upon the altar? Seest thou how

> faith wrought with his works, and by works was faith made perfect? (James 2:21, 22).

The good works that Abraham did here were done through the Holy Spirit, not through the flesh.

> Are ye so foolish? *having begun in the Spirit, are ye now made perfect by the flesh?* (Gal. 3:3).

James never meant for anyone to think man was justified by works before God. If this had been his intention, he would never have included verse 23:

> And the scripture was fulfilled which saith, *Abraham believed God, and it was imputed unto him for righteousness:* and he was called the Friend of God (James 2:23).

Let's take a quick look at a short passage in Romans:

> For what saith the scripture? Abraham *believed* God, and it was counted unto him *for righteousness.* Now to him that worketh is the reward *not reckoned of grace, but of debt.* But to him that worketh not, but *believeth* on him that justifieth the ungodly, *his faith is counted for righteousness* (Rom. 4:3-5).

A person who tries to work his way into God's presence only puts himself deeper in debt to sin. Abraham believed in God and it was counted to him for righteousness, but by his works was he justified in the eyes of men. Good works are a demonstration of the faith that justifies.

> Ye see then how that by works a man is justified, and not by faith only (James 2:24).

In James 2:25, 26 we have a similar situation recorded. A woman was justified by her works before men, but it was her faith that made her right with God. A faith that does not result in one wanting to serve the Lord is lifeless and powerless. Read again the story found in Luke 7:36-50. It was the faith of the woman that saved her, but outward actions gave glory to God before men. If we have truly trusted Jesus to forgive our sins so that we can come into the Father's presence, then we ought to try to maintain good works; not to save us, but to show to the world the love we have for the Savior Who died for us and paid for our sins (1 Cor. 6:19, 20).

I agree with you completely about Matthew 7:21:

Jesus saith unto him, I am the way, the truth, and the life: *no man cometh unto the Father, but by me* (John 14:6).

Verily, verily, I say unto you, He that heareth my word, and *believeth* on him that sent me, *hath everlasting life*, and *shall not come into condemnation;* but *is passed from death unto life* (John 5:24).

We are confident, I say, and willing rather to be absent from the body, and to be present with the Lord (2 Cor. 5:8).

(For he saith, I have heard thee in a time accepted, and in the day of salvation have I succoured thee: *behold, now is the accepted time; behold, now is the day of salvation*) (2 Cor. 6:2).

Boast not thyself of tomorrow; for thou knowest not what a day may bring forth (Prov. 27:1).

He that *believeth* on the Son hath *everlasting life:* and he that *believeth not* the Son *shall not see life; but the wrath of God abideth on him* (John 3:36).

And as it is appointed unto men once to die, but after this *the judgment* (Heb. 9:27).

For *whosoever* shall *call upon the name of the Lord shall be saved* (Rom. 10:13).

Sincerely in prayer,

John Rogers

"Not every one that saith unto me, Lord, Lord, shall enter into the kingdom of heaven; but he that doeth the will of my Father which is in heaven." What is the will of the Father? Jesus stated it in John 6:40:

> And *this is the will of him that sent me,* that every one which seeth the Son, and *believeth on him, may have everlasting life:* and I will raise him up at the last day.

Many people today want to know how they can do the works that God wants them to do to get into His presence. The answer is in John 6:28, 29:

> Then said they unto him, What shall we do, that we might work the works of God? Jesus answered and said unto them, *This is the work of God,* that ye *believe* on him whom he hath sent.

Karen, you have constantly in your letter told me that what you believe is true. That is your privilege, and I would fight for your right to believe as you do. It is important, though, that you understand what the Bible says. You can believe something is true, but that does not make it true. Listen to these verses:

> If we receive the witness of men, *the witness of God is greater:* for this is the witness of God which he hath testified of his Son. He that *believeth* on the Son of God hath the witness in himself: he that *believeth* not God hath made him a liar; because he *believeth* not the record that God gave of his Son. And this is the record, that God hath given to us eternal life, *and this life is in his Son.* He that hath the Son *hath life;* and he that hath not the Son of God *hath not life.* These things have I written unto you that *believe* on the name of the Son of God; *that ye may know that ye have eternal life,* and that ye may *believe* on the name of the Son of God (1 John 5:9-13).

Karen, this has been a long letter, but it has been worth it. I want you to read this letter over again; check out each reference; examine each reference; study each one in context; but do not ignore these references! It is my prayer, Karen, that you will trust the Lord Jesus and Him alone to save you from God's wrath, which the Bible describes as the literal place of hell. If you trust Jesus to save you, He will take you into the presence of God, the Father, when you die. I am waiting anxiously for your reply.